Es   ms

y

98

Published in 1991 by The Rosen Publishing Group, Inc.
29 East 21st Street, New York, NY 10010

First Edition

Manufactured in the United States of America

Library of Congress Cataloging-in Publication Data

Planet earth : egotists and ecosystems.
    p.   cm.   — (Icarus world issues series)
  Includes bibliographical references and index.
  Summary: A collection of fictional and non-fictional stories and essays
dealing with the environment, including its destruction, protection, and
human impact.
    ISBN 0-8239-1334-1 (hardcover)
       0-8239-1335-X (paperback)
    1. Ecology—Literary collections. 2. Pollution—Literary collections.
3. Man—Influence on nature—Literary collections. 4. Environmental
policy—Literary collections. [1. Ecology—Literary collections. 2.
Pollution—Literary collections. 3. Man—Influence on nature—Literary
collections. 4. Environmental policy—Literary collections.] I. Series.

  PZ5.P664 1991
  809'.93355—dc20   91-875
                                                       CIP
                                                        AC

CONTENTS

Introduction

Garbage, profit, miracles, politics, mystery, deception, criminality, and apocalypse are just a few of the themes you'll find in this fourth volume of *Icarus*. For a book series devoted to bringing you the most significant voices and visions from around the world, perhaps no single topic can inspire the degree of urgency and passion from our contributors as the fate of the planet.

From Bali to the Amazon; from Boston to Bangkok, stories and articles have arrived in our offices that have responded to the sacrileges committed against the environment. Had we been presented with impassioned diatribes, the level of our authors' indignation would probably have justified the delivery. The writing in *Icarus* 4, however, is of a different order—the evocation of lost worlds, endless folly, personal courage, and community resistance is rendered with such a subtle palette that the complexity of the issues and our involvement with them belie mere knee-jerk lament.

Sometimes one wishes we were linked to each other solely through bonds of affection and advanced telecommunication, but to these various circuitries we must add the detritus of our consumption and ambition. One person's urban-renewal utopia is another's lost architectural treasure; the rancher who dreams of pastures in the Amazon threatens to scorch the rest of us through his wanton deforestation; a cabal of *apparatchiki* divert water for their newly built summer homes and deprive the shrinking Aral Sea of one of its much needed sources; the pesticides poisoning today's migrant farm workers arrive the next day on America's breakfast tables. Ecological interdependence gives new meaning to our traditional notions of the domino effect.

Our authors come together for the first time in the pages of *Icarus*. Had they had occasion to meet elsewhere—on the fringes of the sahel between Senegal and Mauritania for instance, or on a bus through the hot Oklahoma countryside, or in a bar in Anchorage, there is certainly much that they would have found in common. Nigerian journalist Bunmi Makinwa who writes on Japanese agricultural aid in West Africa would have understood immediately the ironies of American Jonathan Franzen's fiction. German journalists Armin Mahler and Richard Rickelmann who interview Jürgen Strube of the giant German chemical firm BASF would have had no problem in recognizing the personal agenda that Brazilian journalist Lúcio Flávio Pinto encountered in his meeting with rancher and developer Celestino Ribeiro. Russian correspondent Svetlana Vishnevskaya would certainly have found a kindred spirit when hearing about Native American Linda Hogan's ancestral beliefs. Thai writer Charunee Normita Thongtham would have looked through the viewfinder of J. B. McCourtney's camera and seen in the fruit fields of Florida a version of exploitation still to be invented in the Isan region.

Clearly our connections, then, sometimes go beyond affection, and the phone lines, and our garbage to find resonance in the printed word and a shared desire to nurture what we have, what is left.

Roger Rosen, Editor

THE PAINTED
ALPHABET

DIANA DARLING

Diana Darling is an American sculptor whose studies carried her to Paris, France, and Carrara, Italy. In 1980 she traveled to Bali on holiday and soon decided to stay. She lived in a grass hut in the rice fields of Ubud for her first five years there, and it was during that time that she first came across the traditional Balinese tale "Dukuh Siladri" on which her forthcoming novel, *The Painted Alphabet*, is based.

The following selection is an excerpt from *The Painted Alphabet*, which will be published by Houghton Mifflin in March 1992.

Mudita grew up in Mameling in the care of Kompiang and Madé Kerti, believing them to be his real parents, and he did not lack anything his real parents would have given him. From Madé Kerti he learned to grow rice and build walls and play a variety of musical instruments. From Kompiang he learned to be courteous and helpful, and brave in the face of suffering. It was from Ni Sabuk, his grandmother, that he learned about the larger things of the world.

"We are Balinese, Mudita," she told him, "that is, human beings. Our work is to take care of life in the world."

"How big is the world, Nini?"

"Oh, very big—much bigger than Mameling. There are the mountains far to the north, and the sea far to the south. The mountains are the beginning of all things, and the sea is the end of all things."

"And we're in the middle?"

"Yes, we are. Right in the middle of it all. Here we have everything we need."

Mudita was a happy child. He was well loved in the village and had many friends, not only among the boys of his own age, but also among small children and the elderly as well.

He was also an exceptionally beautiful boy. He had inherited his mother's silky skin and enchanting smile; but what distinguished his own special beauty were the legibility of his face and the sweetness of character that lighted it. He had, within the balance of his features, a peculiarity much prized by the Balinese—a small mole at the outer edge of his right eyebrow, which added an elegant adornment to whatever expression lit his face.

It must be added, too, that his body smelled of cinnamon, and his breath smelled of freshly husked rice. But, best of all, he had no idea that there was anything special about himself at all.

As Mudita was growing up, so too was Mameling.

One day Mudita asked his grandmother, "Nini, is Bali the whole world?"

Ni Sabuk clacked her loom. "In a way. Why do you ask?"

"I saw some strange-looking people coming out of the palace today. I thought they must be sick people asking for help, but somebody said they were tourists—they come from beyond Bali. Is that true, Nini?"

"That could be true."

"But how? You said Bali was the whole world. Are the tourists from outside the world?"

"It's like this, 'Dita," she said, drawing with her finger on the palm of her hand. "The world is like a circle. Here in the center is Bali. Then around Bali is Java; people from Java look like normal human beings. Then all around outside is Holland. The people from there are called Dutch and they are very big and pale, it's true."

"Are they human beings?"

"So they say."

"What were Dutch people doing at the palace?"

"They're all aristocrats," said Ni Sabuk. "They like to travel around staying in palaces."

One day the young prince of Mameling summoned a dozen of the most influential villagers. He told them (after they'd all sipped glasses of coffee and lit up the free cigarettes) something like this:

"The future of Mameling is in tourism. Our foreign guests are powerful people in their own countries. They do us a great honor by showing so much interest in our culture. Do you know what culture is?"

4

There was a short silence.

"Culture is the way we do things. The tourists do things differently; they have a different culture—a very poor one, which is why they are so interested in ours. They have lots of money, yes, but they know nothing about the gods; they can't dance or play music (except for their own sort on radios); they don't understand rice, and many of them don't even eat rice."

This produced a roar of laughter from the men.

"So we have to make the tourists feel welcome and comfortable and provide them with the things they need. Now, what do tourists need? And what can we provide them with?"

A rhetorical pause, while the puzzled group sat waiting.

"They need to buy things. And after they buy things, they need a cold drink of beer. They need to eat and sleep—just as we do, but they need to eat in a tourist way and sleep in a tourist way. And they don't know how to go to the river."

Another roar of laughter.

"They need bathrooms, like the Chinese in Denpasar. We'll talk about all this eating and sleeping and bathing in a minute. Now, what do the tourists want to buy? They will try to buy anything, everything. But we're poor people! [This was another rhetorical device; the prince was in fact very rich, and it was the villagers who were poor. No one dared to mention this, of course.] We must use our heads and our hands to make things for the tourists to buy. Some of us can paint—let's make paintings for the tourists. Some of us can carve—let's make sculpture for the tourists . . . or jewelry, if we're good at that. Perhaps our children can dance. Let's have them dance for the tourists! But let us protect our heirlooms. Don't sell your krises.* Don't sell your silver offering bowls and the fine old carvings from your house temples. Let us protect our heritage, our *culture!*"

---

*kris—a short sword or heavy dagger with a wavy blade.

They let this pass, too. It was well known that the prince had made spectacular sales of palace treasures.

"Now. How do we make the tourists comfortable? We all have a bit of extra space in our compounds to build a guest house. How do we do this? First, we get a license, and then we build a nice little house and put in a new bed—it must be new, with a new mattress, pillow, and blanket—and on the porch we give them a chair to sit on. That's right, a chair, just like the one I'm sitting on, but it doesn't have to be as nice as this one—this is from the court in Yogyakarta and is three hundred years old [actually it was Dutch, from Denpasar, circa 1912]. You can put a nice little bamboo chair on the porch for your tourist and a nice little bamboo table for his glass of tea."

One of the men asked the prince if he could explain about the bathroom.

"Very important. It has to be inside the little guest house. That's right, they want the bathroom indoors. And nobody in your family may use it when you have your tourist living there. And you must give your tourist his own private towel. Now here's how it works . . ."

And so Mameling entered the age of "cultural tourism." Soon foreigners were seen everywhere, standing in people's way at the market, milling around in the temples, walking half-undressed and sweaty through the country-side, and forever holding black boxes in front of their faces. The foreigners were ugly, but they were very friendly and hilariously stupid, particularly with their money, of which they seemed to have unlimited amounts. All of this meant great changes for Mameling.

The village became a small town. It joined the great Republic of Indonesia, and representatives came from the government to pave the roads, install electricity, and build clinics and schools. A television was set up on a pole in front of the post office. Somebody bought a refrigerator and an ice-making box, and then somebody else did, and then one villager bought his own private television, and the very next day the prince also bought his own private television, and the race was on.

Meanwhile the tourists were pouring in, and people in Mameling were making a lot of money. Those who could paint, did; and those who couldn't, bought cheap and sold high, and still the tourists were delighted with their bargains. Little girls became little *legong* dancers and grew into big *legong* dancers, and more than one eloped with an enchanted tourist, bringing riches and heartache to her family. "Homestays" suddenly appeared in every backyard and soon materialized in the rice fields, like big, luxurious rice granaries. Some of the old people objected to having toilets in rice granaries, but the younger people explained that they weren't actually rice granaries—they just looked like them because that's what the tourists wanted.

"Who'd want to sleep in a stuffy place like that with all those bugs?" marveled the old people.

"Oh, but it's very nice up there, come look," said the young people.

"Ha! I wouldn't go up there and stand higher than the shrines. Take your own chances."

One old quarter that had always been known as Abian Cheleng [Pig-fields] prospered so quickly that its residents decided to change its name to Tumbensugih [which is Balinese for nouveau riche]. The richest man of Tumbensugih was Gde Kedampal, who as a young boy had been a porter. By working hard and saving carefully, he was able to buy materials to make a pushcart. Soon he had a minivan and married a local girl. When his son, Wayan Buyar, was learning to walk, Gde Kedampal already had three vans, with three paid drivers. By the time Wayan Buyar lost his virginity (to a goose), Gde Kedampal had a prosperous transport business, with a fleet of air-conditioned buses. Later he branched out into packing and shipping.

Many *warungs*—little stands, sometimes no more than little tables, where one can buy rice, coffee, cigarettes, arak, candy, and all sorts of lovely, unhealthy things— became *rumah makan* (Indonesian diners), and they all served cold beer, fried chicken, and "Indonesian Favorites" and "Western Favorites" with imaginative spellings. The Balinese found this food revolting, but they served it cheerfully and made friends with the tourists. Mudita shyly practiced his English with the tourists he met at the traditional *warungs*.

For *warungs* persisted, as did much of the old way of life. People still communed with the gods and held huge, complicated rituals; they still plowed their fields with cows and cooked their rice over smoky wood fires. Madé Kerti and Kompiang watched the world changing beyond their house gates, but life within the compound was much the same, except that their oil lamps were replaced by naked lightbulbs so that Mudita could study more easily in the evenings.

"Ah, technology is a wonderful thing," said Madé Kerti every time he switched on the lights. "You know, 'Piang," he said to his wife one evening, "we're very lucky that the tourists have come to Mameling."

"Is that so," snapped Kompiang. "How, exactly?"

"Look at all the progress they've brought! Lights! Roads! Schools! Don't think it's like this everywhere in Bali."

"The tourists built the roads? I didn't see that."

"No, of course not, they didn't build the roads themselves; our government did, so the tourists could get here more easily—"

"—and raise the price of everything beyond reach and teach our young people to drink beer and wear trousers—"

"Does Mudita drink beer?" said Madé Kerti, suddenly anxious.

"Ask him."

"Mudita! Mudita, darling, come here, just for a minute."

Mudita stood up in the patch of light where he had been studying and walked over to the east pavilion where Madé Kerti and Kompiang were sitting comfortably in the gloom. Mudita sat between his parents.

"Yes, Bapa?" He gave Madé Kerti a beautiful smile.

"Mudita, have you ever had beer?"

"Oh, yes! But it has to be very cold or it's not so nice."

"Mudita, forgive me if I ask you this, but where do you get the money to buy beer? Do you know that a bottle of beer costs almost as much as your mother makes at the market in a whole day?"

"Oh, but I don't buy it—I'm invited by my friends."

"What friends are these?"

Kompiang cut in. "Tourists! Mudita, last night when you came home your breath stank. I don't want you to smell like a tourist."

Madé Kerti put his arm around Mudita's neck. "I'm glad you have generous friends, 'Dita. But just this, to please your mother: After you've been with the tourists, brush your teeth. Okay? Now don't look so sad."

Mudita took Kompiang's hand and pressed it to his face.

"Mudita," Kompiang said. "Don't cry, my baby, I'm not angry with you. I'm not angry. Come here."

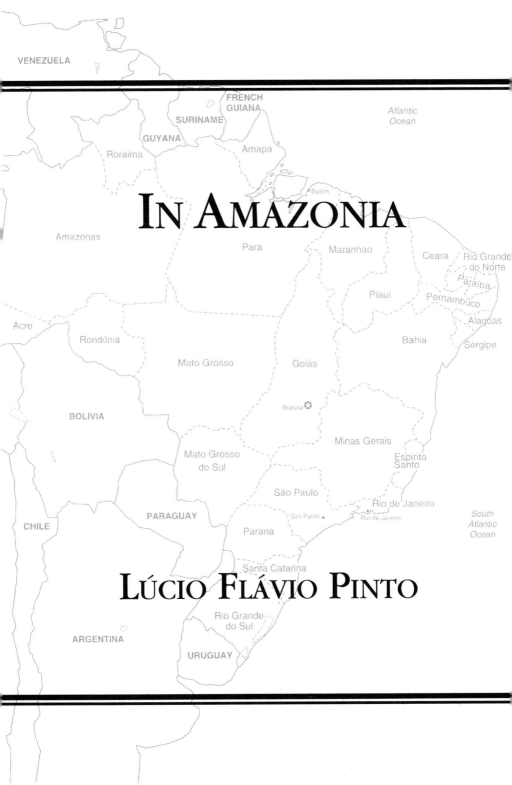

IN AMAZONIA

LÚCIO FLÁVIO PINTO

Lúcio Flávio de Faria Pinto is a Brazilian journalist, writer, and sociologist. He was four times awarded the highest journalistic honor in Brazil, the Prêmio Esso do Jornalismo. In 1983-84 he was a visiting professor at the University of Florida, and since 1990 he has been the director of Amazonian Studies at the Federal University of Pará. He is the author of four books and countless articles.

Mr. Pinto lives in Brazil with his wife, Lenil, and three children, Juliana, Livio, and Angelim.

The well-heeled man seated before me peered out of his office window as he spoke, surveying the flow of traffic some 200 feet below. The intensity of his gaze suggested that he was somehow responsible for its progress. This intensity animated his face anew when the conversation turned to the subject of São Paulo, industrial center of South America, and to the Amazon rain forest 1,900 miles to the north, the last great Brazilian frontier.

Celestino Ribeiro, whom I had come to interview, was a developer from São Paulo, the head of an engineering firm and of a large cattle ranch in Pará, the westernmost district of Amazonia. I was interviewing Ribeiro because developers such as he—a descendant of the *bandeirantes* who tamed Brazil's wilds from the 16th to the 18th centuries, were opening up the wilds of Amazonia. Classical Amazonia, comprising the Brazilian states of Acre, Amapá, Amazonas, Pará, Rondonia, and Roraima, is an area of almost 2.5 million square miles and occupies more than half of northern Brazil.

In 1971, when the process of Amazonian development was still in its early stage, we sat in his luxurious office in downtown São Paulo, one of the most populous cities of the world. That year would mark the formal beginning of the Trans-Amazonian Highway and the colonization of the land along its shoulders. Government propaganda proclaimed the Trans-Amazonian among the greatest human achievements in conquering unknown frontiers, second only to the moon flight by the United States. From the height of their orbit American astronauts would see the two objects on earth that indicate human presence: the Great Wall of China, a utopian project constructed to repel invasions by barbarians, and the Trans-Amazonian, a swath of roadway tearing through the rain forest and opening up land for occupation by the new colonizers. Lying at the very heart of the *sertao*, or hinterlands, the rain forest had until then proven invulnerable.

Ribeiro, brimming with theories about the new world of conquest, was a representative of the group of new colonizers. In order to plant grass and put some livestock in a pasture, self-willed men such as he were chopping down 400- to 500-year-old trees, 130 to 165 feet in height, in a forest whose density—300 to 500 trees per hectare* — is without rival. Pioneers in Brazil had always conducted themselves in this fashion. From the first moment of Portuguese colonization in the 16th century they destroyed the forest, which would later be replaced by desert or savannahs. The *bandeirantes'* 20th-century equivalents were not now going to modify these proven practices in a region that they considered their own by right of conquest. If allowed, they would transform Amazonia into the new São Paulo, a state that by 1971 retained only 8% of its original vegetation.

In fact, Ribeiro was not acquainted with Amazonia, which I verified as the conversation went on. The world of torrential rivers had nothing to do with the urban vision that this man wanted to mold with his strong hands: He would follow the thread reddened by the roadways, reddened in the green mosaic by the regular passing of vehicles that raised dust and gave access to men who wanted to fell the trees.

An imposing man of slow speech and thick eyebrows, Ribeiro was among the most illustrious members of the powerful Association of Developers of Amazonia. The organization had been founded in São Paulo by plantation owners and authorized by the Superintendency for the

---

* Hectare—10,000 square meters, almost 2.5 acres.

Development of Amazonia (SUDAM), a federal authority similar to the Tennessee Valley Authority of the Roosevelt New Deal era. SUDAM itself was created in 1966 to replace another body, the Superintendency for a Plan for the Economic Valuation of Amazonia (SPVEA), which in 1953 had initiated plans for developing the region.

The principal aim of SPVEA had been to introduce industry into Amazonia as though it were a country within a country. This strategy made sense. Since the beginning of the 17th century Amazonia had existed in virtual isolation from the rest of the new country. Under Portuguese rule, authorities in Portugal had directly controlled the region. Indeed, the colonial presence was so strong that Amazonia was finally freed of Portuguese control only in 1835, thirteen years after the rest of Brazil had secured its independence. The Amazonian revolution, the *Cabanagem*, lasted five years and resulted in the death of 30,000 Amazonians, one-fifth of the region's population.

A century later Amazonia attracted international attention by furnishing the Allies with rubber during World War II. The Brazilian government created SPVEA in 1953 precisely to increase the value of the sparsely populated rubber-producing region (having less than one person per square kilometer), distant as it was from the more active national economic centers, difficult to reach, and known for the backward life-styles of its inhabitants. The region was dominated by the most extensive tropical forests in the world, by a vast drainage basin that collects 20% of all fresh water on earth, and by a strong tradition of folklore that influenced how the indigenous peoples made use of the natural resources.

By 1966, the year SUDAM took over, the effects of SPVEA's involvement were already evident. The first open highways permitted land access to Amazonia, previously accessible only by boat or airplane. Brazilians began to buy land at a cost 20 to 30 times cheaper than land in their home states, and to build plantations. People like Celestino Ribeiro. Dozens of São Paulo farmers and industrialists—some people being both—had purchased vast expanses of rain forest and would later turn them into cattle ranches at little economic risk to themselves, taking advantage of grant money offered by the government.

Mere approval of a project by SUDAM guaranteed that a landowner would receive funds from the government, as much as 75% of the money necessary to plant a plantation of 30 or 40 thousand hectares. The grant money was given with the understanding that it would be returned to the government only when, or if, the undertaking turned a profit, and it would be repaid in the form of dividend payments rather than in regular monthly installments. But the projects rarely turned a profit, even if they did reach the planting stage, and most never fully got on track. This was generally attributed to the natural difficulties of Amazonia—the jungle or "green hell," a nature hostile to civilization. Almost two billion dollars left the public coffers to assist in the development of these plantations and ranches, money that never returned, making the rich southern developers even richer.

I had been born in a central district of Amazonia twenty-two years before and had always loved the region. Life, until adolescence, had taught me that Amazonia was a gift of the forest, in the same way that Egypt was a product of the Nile. Without the moisture released by the trees to produce clouds and rain, without their decaying leaves to fertilize the soil, which in turn nourishes the manifold fauna, without the foliage of the treetops to produce chlorophyll and reduce the impact of heavy rain on the earth by protecting it from erosion—without this, what would be left of Amazonia? But man would have to destroy the forest before he could appreciate this fragile balance and find his place in the scenario.

16

Like many inhabitants of the poor North, I had found myself on scholarship in rich São Paulo to go to college. In 1971 I was finishing a double degree in sociology and politics and about to begin graduate school. I already had my dissertation topic in mind: to show that conservative Brazilian thinkers in the 1920s and '30s had been able to develop practical, if flawed, modernization plans for Brazil simply because they were acquainted with the country, whereas most Brazilian intellectuals were too hamstrung by development theories and stereotypes to suggest much of anything.

On that morning in 1971 I fell into a panic. To raise a new world in his own image and likeness, the man behind the desk would destroy the world of my childhood and youth. Ribeiro and men like him were unfeeling conquistadors, barbarians, for whom the Trans-Amazonian, in contrast to the useless Great Wall of China, would serve as a means of draining the area of its rich resources. The developers' economic and political pull virtually guaranteed that they would succeed in imposing their way, which had nothing to do with the wishes of the inhabitants of the region. Nor were their plans informed by the physical characteristics of the area. This man and others like him did not want to hear or to learn. They planned to dominate, using their strongboxes and preconceived notions, their plans in place before they even reached Amazonia. They would repeat there what white colonizers—Belgian, Dutch, English, French, German, Italian, Portuguese, and Spanish—had done in Africa and Asia. Amazonia would be theirs; to the natives would go the leftovers of the banquet, if any were to be had. Ribeiro was a *bwana* * and I an impotent native.

My disillusioning interview in the office of Celestino Ribeiro, whom the American writer Sinclair Lewis

---

* *bwana*—Portuguese for "master."

certainly would have called a plutocrat, changed the direction of my life. I determined to harness my intelligence in passionate service of a project that would benefit Amazonia, a project comprehensible to those who lived there and not meant to assist the new conquistadors. I abandoned the academic path that, two years before, had caused me to trade Belém, the largest city in Amazonia, for São Paulo. Also forfeited was a promising future in journalism, which I had begun to practice professionally in 1966.

This was, coincidentally, the year in which the federal government began to use all of its resources, financial and political, to support the history that the São Paulo "pioneers" and others wanted to write in my native land. In my conversation with Ribeiro, I had come to realize that this history would be written with blotches and errors, pages and pages bearing our signature but not written by us. This history was already showing its horrible effects in Africa and Asia.

By one of the ironies with which history is prolific, I returned to my native Pará as a correspondent for *O Estado de S. Paulo* [The State of São Paulo]. The most influential Brazilian newspaper, it became an intransigent defender of the policy of rapid occupation of the Amazon frontier after "pioneers" from São Paulo had taken the first intrusive steps toward developing the felled forests, an impetus for further development. I was already familiar with a good part of the journalistic milieu, but I still needed to understand the social dynamic, the economic process, and the meandering political interactions that were undoing the thin partitions that barely separated the government bureaus from private offices. The bureaus were ideological, political, or bureaucratic extensions of the latter. Since the government, even when it speaks on behalf of the captains of industry, seems to speak for all, it was imperative that the government participate in the development of Amazonia, even though it be little more than a ventriloquist's dummy. Amazonians thought that the financial leaders of their region were the celebrated personalities in the social columns of provincial newspapers and that the rhythm of life remained that of the past—a patient wait for the fish hiding below in the water, the slow collection of fruits and seeds that fell from the trees, the extraction of sap from the rubber tree. They did not realize that in the middle of the 1950s Amapá, a northeastern state within Amazonia, had begun to export manganese, indispensable for steelmaking and much needed by the United States, the world's major steel producer. From that moment on, some of Brazil's principal economic agents realized that Amazonia was not merely a receptacle for fantastic folklore: It could generate raw materials for products, products of great importance to international economics, not just a reserve for the future.

Amazonians were altogether unaware of what was occurring under their noses; they failed to recognize the advent of a compulsory modernization that would transform everything, overriding them, Africanizing them. Rare indeed were individuals who had the opportunity to participate in a conversation so instructively unnerving as mine in São Paulo. I determined to investigate, disclose, and denounce what I termed "Operation Amazonia," orchestrated and executed by developers without the participation or consultation of the people of Amazonia.

I left Pará and the civilized banks of the Amazon River, where for three centuries Europeans had concentrated on transforming the natural world, and I traveled to the distant, isolated, and sometimes inaccessible economic enterprises of the new colonizers, to the central regions rife with mines. Brazilian intellectuals preferred to continue their speculations in the comfort of the large cities of the region, along the coast or at river junctions, ignoring the

19

highlands of the *sertao*. They grappled with the most forward-looking theories but turned their backs on the terrible history that was then taking root in the *sertao*. They would become aware that history was in the making only when the echo of barbarism resounded at their gates. The warning signal was the suddenly accelerated pace at which the rain forest was being leveled. What would the world do if it were known that the Egyptians were going to destroy the Nile (as they had threatened to do in the 1950s with the construction of the Aswan Dam)? That was more or less what Brazilians were doing to Amazonia. In 1972, at a global conference on development and ecology sponsored by the United Nations, representatives from around the world had affirmed that nature was not a passive guinea pig for human experimentation. Nature was suffering at the hands of humans but would avenge itself, and humankind would suffer with it.

When I returned to Amazonia I witnessed savagery that harkened back to primitive times. Wherever there was an open roadway, one would see numerous sites where fire was consuming the foliage, sometimes with no activity to follow the ashes. The forest, center and source of life for the region, was not only of no value to the São Paulo developers, it was an obstacle. Instead of trees, they wanted pastureland, cultivated areas, streets, cities, hydroelectric plants—everything that would facilitate the manufacture of merchandise desired by buyers from other states and especially from abroad. Only those who destroyed the foliage had the right to a piece of land; that was government policy, a policy that portended disaster for the indigenous peoples.

Homo sapiens had brightened neolithic caves with fire, the first tool of economic transformation. Fire would also be the principal weapon of the developers of Amazonia. In 1975 it was necessary to resort to the most sophisticated machinery, the information satellite, to quantify destruction of the region by fire. In that year deforestation had struck only 0.8% of Amazonia. Euclides da Cunha, a great Brazilian writer who visited the region at the beginning of the century, had said that Amazonia was a page not written in Genesis, that God had transferred it to humankind to make of it whatever they would. Euclides had been struck by the immaturity, even geological, of a region at once monumental and fragile that was still forming itself. It was still a virtual blank page in 1975.

But in 1987 when a satellite again "photographed" the region, the destruction already exceeded 7% of Amazonia, a devastated area the size of France. Throughout the '80s the extent of the destruction by burning of the forest was 12,500 to 19,000 square miles per year, or roughly 35 to 50 square miles per day. Never before had man destroyed so much. Such ferocity had an explanation: Amazonia had to yield materials as rapidly as possible for sale on the international market. That was the only way for the country to acquire dollars to make payments on its enormous international debt of $120 billion, larger than any other country's.

In fact, Amazonia had responded generously to this urgent need. At the beginning of the '80s exports from Amazonia totaled $400 million; at the start of the '90s the value was $2 billion. Simultaneously, Amazonia's population jumped from one to six percent of the total population. The region became Brazil's principal source of manganese, bauxite, tin, iron deposits, aluminum, gold, wood, and fish, as well as other essentials and raw materials that manufacturers transformed into finished products, reaping great profits in the process. Of course, this most lucrative step, the manufacture of goods, occurred outside of Amazonia.

As a result, major Amazonian cities with populations of as many as 1.2 million, such as Belém, now have hydro-electric plants that are among the largest in the world as well as ultramodern industries. But one out of every fifty residents has malaria, an endemic fever that multiplies its casualties in the wake of deforestation. Tens of thousands die each year of yellow fever, typhoid fever, polio, measles, diarrhea, and simple starvation. While the gross national product (that popular figure used by economists to calculate national wealth) rose a dramatic 500% over the course of the decade, that had little effect on individual Brazilians; per capita income increased by a slim 1% over the same period because the population grew more quickly than the wealth did. Many Brazilians were drawn to Amazonia by the prospect of amassing wealth quickly but saw their plans fail.

In some Amazonian cities the increase in population has been 20% annually, doubling every five years or less because of migration. But a student of the bloody move West in the 19th-century United States can leave the pages of those history texts and step into the Amazonian present without noticing any difference. In Amazonia, at the very end of the 20th century, at the dawn of a new age marked by the information society, whites kill Indians, who in turn attack and rob trains. Roads are blocked off to slow the passage of vehicles carrying people with .38 revolvers showing conspicuously in their belts. If in Amazonia fire announces economic action, easy death is a mark of the social process. People kill one another without difficulty, with impunity. In the confines of the jungle, life is worth little, almost nothing.

Sixteen years later, in July 1987, I was in the SUDAM auditorium in Belém where people such as Celestino Ribeiro used to go to check on the approval status of their projects. A reporter friend arrived, looking shaken, and whispered in my ear: Paulo Fonteles has been killed.

Two years my senior, Fonteles was an organizer for the Communist Party of Brazil. We had been friends as students, when he had joined the left. Arrested and tortured, he managed to finish his studies only some time after I did and afterward dedicated himself to practicing law in defense of the squatters. Figures largely from the past in the U.S., squatters were assisted through the Homestead Act,* but they were very much alive in the 1980s in the chaotic agrarian structure of Amazonia, a place favorable to the concentration of property in a few hands. Even today, 1% of the property owners control 57% of land in the area.

Through his bravery, which at other times was unproductive, Fonteles got himself elected state representative of Pará as an advocate of farm workers, a social category invariably on the fringes of those favored by the state. But in a violently conservative country that has not yet succeeded in reforming its skewed agrarian structure, Fonteles was unable to win reelection. When he was killed he had returned to being the courageous lawyer of the colonized peoples.

When I reached the gas station on the highway leading out of the city and found his car, his body was still warm. He appeared to be sleeping, his head tilted slightly, his body upright in the front seat, legs crossed, cold cigarette butt between his fingers. The mark that something was wrong was at the back of his neck and by his right ear, three small holes with clotted blood. Only on the other side of his face had the bullets done evident damage as they exited, breaking bones and tearing open flesh. The first of the bullets had killed Paulo Fonteles; the other two were fired only to confirm the "service." Paulo hadn't had a chance to defend himself, perhaps not even to be frightened.

---

* Homestead Act—An Act of Congress of 1852 making public lands in the West available to settlers at no cost.

A seasoned reporter in the backlands of the Amazon, I had seen death. It is impossible not to come into contact with it. The region gives rise to the most primitive and savage form of conflict resolution, murder, as primitive and savage as the fire that consumes the forest. In the last ten years 700 union leaders, lawyers, priests, and workers have been killed on the dirt roads that serve the pioneering fronts. There is always someone who wants to eliminate someone else; thus the permanent presence of one or two thousand professional gunslingers available to execute a disliked or inconvenient person for less than $100. Not even in the Wild West was a hired gun so cheap.

The body of Paulo Fonteles in front of me, however, revealed to what lengths disrespect for human life could go. Until then, assassins had made it a practice to await their victims in the jungle, respecting certain civilizing limits. But now they had liquidated a citizen at the only exit from the largest city of the region, and it seemed that they were going to escape without penalty, as always. I promised myself that this time would be different.

I spent the following three months investigating the assassination. I found myself suddenly alone and well ahead of the police, who were standing in place. I was also well beyond the willingness of the press to make use of my information. It strongly implicated local millionaires in plotting Fonteles' murder, or at least in covering it up, and revealed a chain of violence with connections reaching into the chambers of the very government that had only recently ended the police state era.

To be able to publish this information (nothing more than information), I had to found a newspaper, write it entirely on my own, and depend on only my family to deliver it to readers. Suggestively, I named it "Personal Journal," an eight-page biweekly newsletter the size of a notice, and maintained it for 66 editions over three years.

During this time I stayed poor, investing whatever resources I had into the paper. I was pressured, threatened with death, and entirely worn out personally. I had the sad privilege of publishing, always alone, the sad facts such as diversion of public monies, corruption, organized crime, influence peddling, the ruin of nature, crooked deals, administrative irregularities, and political coups, and a series of profiled crimes (never denied) that should have brought the accused to the gates of justice but did not. In the beginning of 1991 I reached my limit for single-handedly sustaining the publication and brought it to a close.

Now I am again involved in a journalistic project, this time directing a larger newspaper, more aggressive, capable of exerting a deeper influence. Twenty years after having decided to return to Amazonia to follow its history, record it, and try to give it a direction more in keeping with the desires of its people, I worry about the results that will be gained. From being a highly honored journalist, with easy access to the largest papers, I turned myself into a marginal, a professional who creates his own margin for expression on the margin of the already established margin.

It is said that I am the person who best knows Amazonia, and so I am invited to conferences in various parts of the country and outside as well. But despite my efforts, successive years have not improved prospects for my region. To stare along the past is to recall martyrs, but to project the future fails to feed our hopes. Not a few people, even those on the sidelines at greater or lesser distances, have been affected by the violence disseminated throughout the region. The cases of those killed or silenced are only the most explicit expression of the imposed vision, that of a forcibly occupied and developed Amazonia, a history revisited from the colonial African and Asian pasts. Many are those against whom I promised myself to do battle and, after a quarter of a century, was not able to overcome. Not I, nor those who here planted their dreams, rocked by the many surprises that the Amazon adventure produces in those who, in spite of all, do not lose the sensitivity and the desire to think and to dream.

Translated by Charles Martin

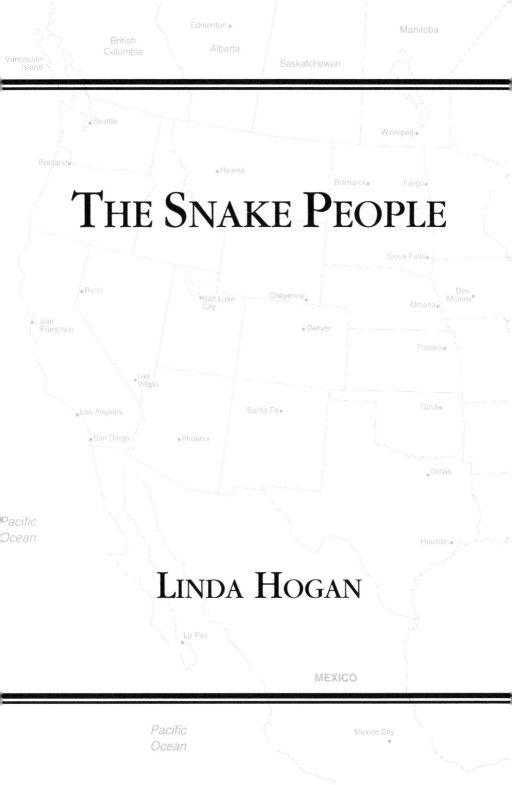

THE SNAKE PEOPLE

LINDA HOGAN

Linda Hogan is a Chickasaw poet, novelist, and essayist. She is the author of several books of poetry. Her novel *Mean Spirit* was awarded the 1990 Oklahoma Book Award for Fiction. Her collection of poems, *Seeing Through the Sun*, received an American Book Award from the Before Columbus Foundation. Ms. Hogan has received writing grants from the National Endowment for the Arts and the Minnesota Arts Board as well as a Colorado Writer's Fellowship and a 1992 Guggenheim Fellowship. She is also the recipient of the Five Civilized Tribes Museum playwriting award. Her forthcoming book, Red Clay, a collection of poetry and fiction, will be published by Greenfield Review Press.

Ms. Hogan is an associate professor at the University of Colorado, where she teaches in the Creative Writing program. She has served on the poetry panel for the National Endowment for the Arts for the past two years and is a volunteer on behalf of wildlife rehabilitation.

One green and humid summer my father and I were driving through the hot Oklahoma countryside. I had just handed over the wheel of the truck to him and was bathing my face with a wet cloth when something that looked like a long golden strand of light leapt up, twisted in the wavering air, and flew lightning fast across the road. We stopped, both of us jumping out, in time to see the golden racer vanish into the kingdom of roots and soil.

That flying snake, that thin flash of light, brought back a store of memories. Our lives have been peopled with snakes and stories of snakes: there was my Chickasaw grandfather who, riding his stocky, thick-muscled horse, could smell the reptile odor from a distance and thus keep his horse away from rattlers curled beneath rocks or stretched out in the warm sun. And my Aunt Louise had a reputation for swimming among water moccasins so smoothly that they did not take note of her. Then there was the time my father and I were digging for fishing worms when we came across an abandoned well.

The well was in the middle of a dry Oklahoma emptiness, where summer heat had cracked the earth into broken tiles of red clay. The well was covered with a plank of wood, a heavy stone placed on top to hold it down in windstorms and to keep children my size from falling in. We moved the stone, lifted the wooden lid, and peered down into the cool, dark cistern. It smelled dank and rich, a welcome moisture in the hot summer. It was lined with round stones all the way down the musty darkness. Inside, not far from the surface of the ground and raising itself out from the stones, a blue racer glided into the newly lighted air, its tongue calculating the world. Quickly, my father caught it. He held it just behind the head for a while, then put it in my hands, and when we returned to my grandmother's house I was happy thinking of what a big fish we would catch with it. I remember still the gray blue color of it, like a heron, the slenderness, and the dry beauty that wound down toward the dusty ground, wanting to escape me.

There were other stories, those in which snakes were fearsome creatures: a rattlesnake curled around a telephone ready to strike an answering hand, a snake in a swamp cooler, or one that crawled into bed with one of the children. And there was the time my brother woke to feel the weight of a rattlesnake heavy between his knees.

Most of the snakes of my childhood, even those without venom, were greeted by death held in human hands. They were killed with shovels, hoes, sticks, and sometimes with guns. Most people are uneasy about sharing territory with snakes. Last year, hearing a gunshot, I went up the road to see what had happened. A neighbor, shaken, told me that he had heard something on his front porch. At first he thought it was some kind of a motor running, but when he spotted a rattlesnake curled up there, he stole away in search of his rifle and shot it.

Looking back on the blue racer of Oklahoma, that thin pipe of life, I believe that snake, too, must have met its death in our discovery of it. But its graceful life, not its death, is what has remained in my memory. And down through the years I have come to love the snakes and their long, many-ribbed bodies.

Maybe my love was strengthened years ago when I dreamed of a woman who placed a fantastic snake over her face. The snake was green and the woman merged with it, wearing it like a mask, her teeth fitting inside its fangs, her face inside its green beak-like, smooth-scaled face. Her breath became the snake's slow breathing, and they lived through one another, inhabiting a tropical world of wet leaves, vines, and heavy, perfumed flowers. As the woman began to dance, other people emerged from the forest wearing feathers, deep blue and emerald green, like human birds brilliant with the dew on them. They joined the snake woman in a dance, placing their hands on one another's waists the way Chickasaws, my tribe, sometimes dance. Everything became alive with the movement of that dance. But after a while the music became sadder than the jungle and both disappeared a bit at a time behind the large dark leaves, vanishing behind rain into the rich, fertile song of water. The woman removed the snake and placed it on a wall, where it hung alive and beautiful, waiting for another ceremonial dance. The woman said, "All the people have pieces of its skin. If they save the pieces, it will remain alive. If everyone owns it, it will be preserved."

At first I thought this dream was about Indian tradition, how if each person retains part of a history, an entire culture and lifeway remains intact and alive, one thing living through the other like the snake and woman in the dream. But since that time I've expanded my vision. Now it seems that what needs to be saved, even in its broken pieces, is earth itself, the tradition of life, the beautiful blue-green world that lives in the coiling snake of the Milky Way.

It is late spring. Pollen is floating in the air. I am walking up the road when I see an incredible sight. A snake four feet long is stretched out straight as a stick across the road. It sees me coming, or I should say feels me, my feet on the ground, and without winding or curving it moves slowly off the road, remaining straight as the shadow of a fence post. It moves off the road so carefully and mysteriously, an inch at a time, as though sliding off ice. It disappears into the bushes, and by the time I reach the place there is no trace that it has been there. But I stand and listen for it, because a friend who once kept snakes for milking venom told me he located snakes by the whispering sound made as they brushed through the grasses.

He once saw a black racer carried into the sky by a red-tailed hawk. It was alive and whipping through air as it tried to get loose from the sharp claws that held it when another hawk appeared and fought to take the snake from the first. Fighting with beaks and claws, the birds became involved in their hunger struggle, but as they fought the snake came loose and began a steep fall to earth. Seeing it, both hawks forgot their fight and dove straight down after it, but the snake, still twisting, landed in the thick canopy of trees, where it may have found shelter and survived.

I once saw an eagle carrying a snake through the sky to its nest. I wouldn't have noticed it if not for my dog, Annie, who stopped in the road, staring upward with something like awe and surprise in her face. Birds of prey, like those hawks and that eagle, are natural enemies of snakes and can sight them from far off. But another time I saw a snake swallowing a bird, the twig-like feet sticking out of the snake's wide mouth.

At flood time, the vulnerable snakes emerge from rocky ground and move upward to hills and mounds, seeking refuge from the torrential waters that invade their homes. Silver with water, they wind about one another, slide over stones and through mud, and then rise up the rough trunks of trees, where they wrap themselves around branches and wait out the storm. Gold-eyed, they stretch across the limbs, some looping down, some curled tight and nest-like between branch and trunk, their double tongues darting out like weather vanes. They remind me of women who know they are beautiful.

*   *   *

Before Snake became the dark god of the Christian under-world, burdened with human sin, it carried a different weight in our human bones; it was a being of holy inner earth. The smooth gold eye, the hundred ribs holding life, it coiled beautifully and mysteriously around the world of human imagination. In ancient cultures the snake was the symbol of healing and wholeness. Even the old ones, like the Adena people, who left no recorded history, left a tribute to the snake in one of the mounds near Chillicothe, Ohio. Over 1,200 feet in length, the mound is an earth sculpture of an open-mouthed serpent that clasps an egg, a potential for new life, in its jaws. This is only one of many worldwide images of snakes, some curled about an egg, others with tail in mouth, telling us about the germinal beginnings of life and renewal, of infinity gone in a circle round itself.

But in more recent times the snake has symbolized our wrongs, our eating from the tree of knowledge, our search and desire for the dangerous revelations of life's mystery. In only a short span of earth's history the power of that search, the drive toward knowledge, have brought ruin to our Eden. Knowledge without wisdom, compassion, or understanding has damned us as we have been stirring about in the origins of life, breaking apart the miniature worlds of atoms just to see where that breaking will take us.

Every year the Hopi, another indigenous people, whose name means "People of Peace," participate in a snake dance. They have a strong understanding of the snake people who have lived in the land long before humans were here. Snakes are the old ones, immortals who shed a milky skin to reveal the new and shining. For as long as anyone remembers, the cared-for snakes have been fed with pollen, stroked with feathers, placed on a circle of finely ground meal, and then carried into the dance.

Afterwards they are returned unharmed to the thick dry dust and heat of the red land, to the dens they have lived in for thousands and thousands of generations. It is the oldest ritual in the history of our continent, and it is danced by some of the oldest people who have continuously inhabited and grown from this holy land.

Going even deeper, the image of snakes twined about a tree or one another looks surprisingly like the double, twisted helix of DNA, the spiral arrangement of molecules that we share with every other living thing on earth, plant and animal, down to the basic stuff of ourselves. Perhaps Snake dwells at the zero of ourselves, takes us full circle in a return to the oldest knowledge, that which says the earth is alive. Our bodies, if not our minds, know that zero, that core, the constellation of life at our human beginnings, that same shape of the galaxy.

*　*　*

I call them people. That's what they are. They have been here inhabiting the same dens for tens of thousands of generations, threading between rocks, stretching in the sun, disappearing into the grass. They belong here. They love their freedom, their dwelling places, and they often die of what we could call sadness when kept in captivity.

I am walking on the red road when I see the silver snake. It has been hit by a car and is dying, writhing in the place where it has only a moment earlier been full of life and stretched out on the warm, sunny road. Looking close, I notice the slit in the snake's slender belly, a gaping wound. By now the snake is dead. An infant snake is hanging out from that wound. At first I think it is an unborn snake not yet come to life in the world. I am calculating the kind of food I will need for an infant snake, when it comes to me that this snake lays eggs, that this smaller one is not waiting to be born but has been swallowed. Looking closer, I see another fall out the thin sleeve of snake. Still another falls from the dry scales. I tug at it, and several more spill out. It is strange to see them open out that way, as if blooming from the skinny tunnel of what had been alive just a few moments ago. Then—surprise—I see one of them move. It is alive, free of its prison, somehow surviving. It must not yet have passed from the gullet into the stomach's strong digestive fluids. The tiny snake darts away and vanishes into stones and grass. It leaves a winding, thin path in the road dust. Maybe it is writing a story of survival there on the road, of what is left of wilderness, or of what has become of earth's lesser gods as one by one they disappear.

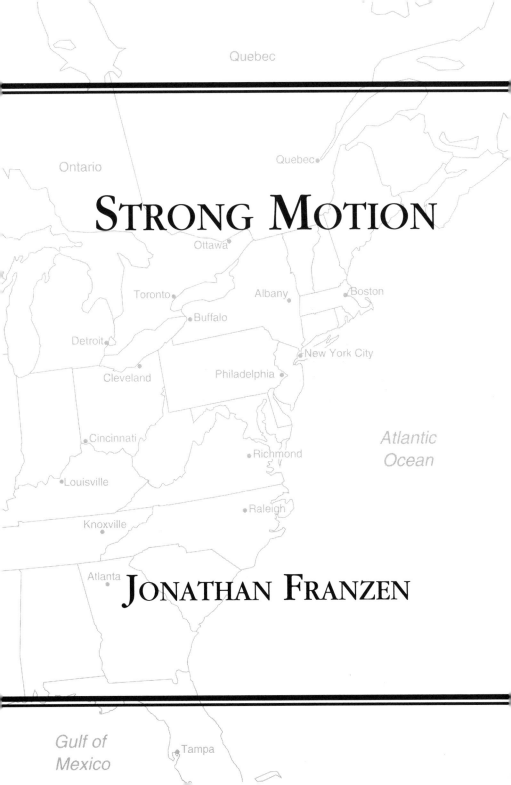

STRONG MOTION

JONATHAN FRANZEN

Jonathan Franzen was raised in St. Louis, Missouri. He attended Swarthmore College and in 1981 was awarded a Fulbright Fellowship to study at the Free University in Berlin. From 1983 to 1987 he was a part-time research assistant at Harvard University, where he analyzed earthquake data.

Mr. Franzen is the author of the novel *The Twenty-Seventh City*. The following selection is an excerpt from his forthcoming novel, *Strong Motion*, which will be published by Farrar, Straus & Giroux in January 1992.

Mr. Franzen and his wife, Valerie Cornell, currently live in Philadelphia and Colorado.

All Monday, all Tuesday, the earthquake held the country hostage. Giant headlines marching lockstep like fascist troops booted everything else off the front pages, and in the afternoon people trying to watch soap operas were subjected to special reports instead. Major-league baseball canceled two nights' worth of games in case fans had any ideas of taking refuge from the news in balls and strikes. Even the Vice President was forced to cut short his swing through Central American capitals and fly to Boston.

It's not pleasant to be held hostage; it's not just a figure of speech. In a decadent society people can slowly drift or can slowly be drawn by the culture of commerce into yearning for violence. Maybe people have a deep congenital awareness that no civilization lasts forever, that the most peaceful prosperity will someday have to end, or maybe it's just human nature. But war can begin to seem like a well-earned fireworks display, and a serial killer (as long as he's in a distant city) like a man to root for. A decadent society teaches people to enjoy advertisements of violence against women, any suggestion of the yanking down of women's bra straps and the seizing of their breasts, the raping of women, the hearing of their screams. But then some woman they know gets abducted and raped and not only fails to enjoy it but becomes angry or is injured for a lifetime, and suddenly they are hostages to her experience. They feel sick with constriction, because all those sexy images and hints have long since become vital bridges to span the emptiness of their days.

And now the disaster which had been promising to make you feel that you lived in a special time, a real time, a time of the kind you read about in history books, a time of suffering and death and heroism, a time that you'd remember as easily as you'd forget all those years in which you had done little but futilely pursue sex and romance through your purchases: Now a disaster of these historic proportions had come, and now you knew it wasn't what you'd wanted either. Not this endless televised repetition of clichés and earnest furrowings of reportorial brows, not these nightmare faces of anchorpeople in pancake staring at you hour after hour. Not this footage of the same few bloody bodies on stretchers. Not this sickening proliferation of identical newspaper interviews with identical survivors who said it was scary and identical scientists who said it was not well understood. Not these photos of buildings that were damaged but not obliterated. Not this same vision, over and over, of the smoking ruin in Peabody on which an ordinary morning sun shone because the sun still rose because the world wasn't changed because your life wasn't changed. You would have preferred the more honest meaninglessness of a World Series, the entertainment of an event toward which months of expectation and weeks of hype could build, bridging a summer and fall's emptiness and producing, in conclusion, an entirely portable set of numbers which the media couldn't rub your face in for more than about an hour. Because you could see now that the earthquake was neither history nor entertainment. It was simply an unusually awful mess. And although the earthquake too could be reduced to a score—injuries 1,300, deaths 71, magnitude 6.1—it was the kind of score that your righteous captors felt justified in repeating until you went insane and screamed a scream which they, behind their microphones and computer monitors, didn't hear.

The picture that made Monday evening's front pages around the world showed the ruins of Sweeting-Aldren's chemical facilities in Peabody. Twenty-three of the deaths and 110 of the injuries had been suffered by company employees caught in the initial explosion of two process lines and the ensuing general conflagration. The earthquake had disabled various fire-control systems, and balls of combusting ethylene and sheets of flaming benzene had ignited storage tanks. A blast apparently caused by ammonium nitrate leveled process lines that otherwise might not have burned. White clouds rained nitric acid and hydrochloric acid and organic reagents, the hydrocarbons and halogens combining in an environment as high-temperature and low-pH as the surface of Venus, but considerably more toxic. Cooling and drifting, the vapor plume descended on residential neighborhoods and left a whitish, oily residue on everything it touched.

By Monday afternoon EPA officials in mylar suits were measuring dioxin levels in the parts-per-hundred-thousand on streets north of the installation. Birds littered the ground beneath trees like fallen, mold-cloaked fruit. Cats and squirrels and rabbits lay dead on lawns or convulsing and retching under hedges. The weather was lovely, temperature in the high seventies, humidity low. National Guard units in tear-gas gear worked methodically northward, evacuating recalcitrant homeowners with force when necessary, barricading streets with orange barrels, and encircling the most contaminated area, designated Zone I, with flimsy orange plastic fencing material that had apparently been stockpiled with this very purpose in mind.

By Tuesday evening Zone I had been completely isolated. It consisted of five and a half square miles of gravel pits, shabby residential streets, trash-glutted wetlands, and some worn-out factories owned by companies that had long been scaling back. Already several Peabody residents who had been at home when the plume descended were in the hospital, complaining of dizziness or extreme fatigue. The houses they had left behind, now visitable only by

41

National Guard patrols and news teams, had the aspect of junked sofas—the bad legs, the weakened joints, the skin torn here and there to expose an internal chaos of springs and crumbled stuffing. Earthquake damage was similar in the much larger Zone II to the north, but here the contamination was spotty and ill defined enough that the Guard was letting adult residents return during daylight hours to secure their houses and collect personal belongings.

News was being gathered in Peabody round the clock. Camera crews skirmished with the Guard, and reporters addressed their audiences in gas masks. Some were so affected by what they had seen, so unexpectedly overwhelmed by the news, that they dropped their pious earnest poses and spoke like the intelligent human beings you'd always figured they had to be. They asked Guardsmen if any looters had been shot. They asked environmental officials if people living just outside the Zones were at risk. They asked everyone what their *impressions* were. But the big question, not only for the press but for the EPA, the 30,000 traumatized and outraged residents of Zones I and II, the citizens of Boston, and all Americans as well, was: What did the management of Sweeting-Aldren have to say? And it was on Monday afternoon, when the question had become inescapable, that the press discovered that there was literally no one in Boston to answer it. Sweeting-Aldren's corporate headquarters, situated, as it happened, just west of Zone II, had been gutted by a fire that local fire departments said appeared to have been arson. The building's sprinkler system had been shut down manually, and firemen found a "flammable liquid" near the remains of the ground-floor records center. The wives of the company's CEO and its four vice-presidents either could not be found or told reporters that they hadn't seen their men since late Sunday evening, shortly before the earthquake struck.

At five o'clock on Monday, just in time for a live interview on the local news, Channel 4 tracked down company spokesman Ridgely Holbine at a marina in Marblehead. He was wearing swim trunks and a faded HARVARD CREW T-shirt and was inspecting his sailboat for earthquake damage.

PENNY SPANGHORN: What is the company's response to this terrible tragedy?

HOLBINE: Penny, I can't give you any official comment at this time.

SPANGHORN: Can you tell us what caused this terrible tragedy?

HOLBINE: I've received no information on that. I can speculate privately that the earthquake was a factor.

SPANGHORN: Are you in communication with the company's management?

HOLBINE: No, Penny, I'm not.

SPANGHORN: Is the company prepared to take responsibility for the terrible contamination in Peabody? Will you take a leading role in the clean-up?

HOLBINE: I can't give you any official comment.

SPANGHORN: What is your personal opinion of this terrible tragedy?

HOLBINE: I feel sorry for the workers who were killed and injured. I feel sorry for their families.

SPANGHORN: Do you feel personally responsible in any way? For this terrible tragedy?

HOLBINE: It's an act of God. There's no controlling that. We all regret the loss of life, though.

SPANGHORN: What about the estimated 30,000 people who are homeless tonight as a result of this tragedy?

HOLBINE: As I said, I have no authority to speak for the company. But it's undeniably regrettable.

SPANGHORN: What do you have to say to those people?

HOLBINE: Well, they shouldn't eat any food from their houses. They should shower carefully and try to find other places to stay. Drink bottled water. Get plenty of rest. That's what I'm doing.

Tuesday morning brought the news that Sweeting-Aldren CEO Sandy Aldren had spent all of Monday in New York City liquidating the company's negotiable securities and transferring every dollar it had in cash to bank accounts in a foreign country. Then, on Monday night, he had vanished. At first it was assumed that the foreign accounts in question were Swiss, but records showed that all the cash—about $30 million—had in fact flowed to the First Bank of Basseterre in St. Kitts.

On Tuesday afternoon Aldren's personal attorney in Boston, Alan Porges, came forward and acknowledged that a "cash reserve" had been set up to cover the "contractually guaranteed severance payments" of the company's five "ranking officers." These payments amounted to just over $30 million, and Porges said that to the best of his knowledge all five officers had officially resigned on Monday morning and were therefore entitled to their cash payments effective immediately. He declined to speculate on the men's whereabouts.

The networks had rebroadcast excerpts from the interview with Porges no more than five or six times when a new bombshell detonated. Seismologist Larry Axelrod summoned reporters to MIT and announced that he had seen evidence indicating that Sweeting-Aldren had been pumping large volumes of chemical waste into a deep well in Peabody, thus making it responsible for nearly all the seismic activity of the last three months, including the main shock on Sunday night. He said the evidence had been provided by Renée Seitchek of Harvard, "an excellent scientist" who was still in the hospital recovering from gunshot wounds. A woman from the *Globe* asked if it was possible that Seitchek had been shot by a Sweeting-Aldren operative, and Axelrod said *yes*.

Police in Somerville and Boston confirmed that they had widened the scope of their investigation of Seitchek's shooting in light of this newfound motive, but added that the earthquake had thrown all investigations into disarray. They said the total breakdown of Sweeting-Aldren's management structure and the loss of company records to various fires "could pose a problem."

Federal and state environmental officials were encountering even bigger obstacles as they attempted to confirm the existence of an injection well at the company's Peabody facilities. By Wednesday morning the last of the fires there had burned itself out, and what remained was 800 acres of scorched and poisoned ruins—an uncharted industrial wasteland filled with murky, foaming pools, unstable process structures, and pressurized tanks and pipelines suspected to contain not only explosives and flammable gases but some of the most toxic and/or carcinogenic and/or teratogenic substances known to man. The EPA's first priority, administrator Susan Carver told ABC News, would be to prevent contamination from spreading into groundwater and nearby estuaries.

"It's now apparent," Carver said, "that this company's immense profitability was achieved through razor-thin safety margins and the systematic deception of the agencies responsible for oversight. I'm afraid there's a very real risk of this personal and economic tragedy becoming a true environmental catastrophe, and right now I'm more worried about protecting public safety than assigning responsibility in the abstract. For us to locate a single wellhead at the site, assuming the well even exists, is going to be like finding a needle in a haystack that we know is full of rattlesnakes."

By and large the press and public bought the Axelrod/Seitchek theory wholesale. Seismologists, however, reacted with their usual caution. They wanted to inspect the data. They needed time to model and construe. They said the rich and swarmy seismicity of April and May could plausibly have been induced by Sweeting-Aldren, but the main shock on Sunday night was another matter.

What was certain was that the eastern United States had suffered its largest earthquake since Charleston, South Carolina, was crunched in 1886. The contamination of Peabody and the scandal of corporate culpability naturally received the most press in the early going—every big American disaster seems to produce one particularly grim spectacle—but as the situation there stabilized, attention shifted to the serious wounds suffered by the rest of north suburban Boston and the city itself. Rescue workers digging in the rubble of a children's home in Salem had exhumed eight small bodies. Heart attacks had killed at least ten Hub men and women; Channel 7 interviewed neighbors of a West Somerville man named John Mullins who had staggered from his house and fallen dead in the street with his arms outstretched "like he'd been shot." Trichlorobenzene pouring out of dry-cleaning establishments had put six people in the hospital. Librarians in every town from Gloucester to Cambridge were wading into hip-deep swamps of unshelved books. Shawmut Bank's mainframe had crashed, and an electrical fire had wiped out hundreds of magnetic tapes containing account information; the bank closed its doors for a week, and its customers, finding that their ATM cards wouldn't work at other banks either, had to barter and beg and borrow just to get food and bottled water. Many people complained of lingering seasickness. After Sunday night only three minor aftershocks were felt, but each of them caused hundreds of people to stop whatever they were doing and sob uncontrollably. Everything was a mess—houses, factories, highways, courts. On Friday morning federal relief coordinators estimated that the total cost of the earthquake, including property damage and the interruption of economic activity, but not including the contamination in Zones I and II, would come to between four and five billion dollars. Editorialists called the figure staggering; it was roughly what it had cost Americans to service the national debt over the Memorial Day weekend.

A season of lawsuits ensued. Lawsuits salved the raw nerves of the million survivors and held out hope to the bereft. They eased the transition back to normalcy when the networks and newspapers released their hostages; they provided the grist for follow-up reports. They bottled the terrible dread and emptiness back into people's unconscious, where they belonged. By the end of July the Commonwealth of Massachusetts had been named in eleven separate suits accusing it of such creative torts as failure to establish adequate plans for evacuation in the event of toxic chemical dispersal, lethargy in providing shelter for families from Zones I and II, and calculated deception in its assessments of local seismic risk. The Commonwealth in turn was suing the federal government and the builders of various failed highways and public buildings. It was also, like nearly everyone else in Boston, suing Sweeting-Aldren. As of August 1 total claims against the company exceeded $10 billion and were rising daily. To pay these claims, the company had no current assets, a long-term debt of $50 million, and little prospect of ever selling anything again. It was taken for granted that the federal government would ultimately foot the clean-up bill.

Authorities were still hoping to bring Sweeting-Aldren's management home to face a variety of criminal charges. The FBI had tracked the five men—Aldren, Tabscott, Stoorhuys, the corporation counsel, and the chief financial officer—to a tiny island south of St. Kitts, where the corporation had long maintained three beach houses for busi-

47

ness entertaining and executive vacations. Aldren's 23-year-old wife, Kim, and Tabscott's 26-year-old girlfriend, Sondra, had joined the party a few days after the earthquake, the corporation counsel's family had visited on the Fourth of July, and seafaring paparazzi had managed to photograph a beach picnic that resembled a beer commercial in all particulars. (The *Globe* ran one of these pictures on its front page alongside a shot of mylar-suited men shoveling birds and mammals into an incinerator.) Unfortunately the government of St. Kitts and Nevis showed no intention of delivering the executives up to justice, and the Administration in Washington, mindful of Aldren and Tabscott's longtime financial support of the Republican Party, said there was little the United States could do about it.

Big chemical concerns like Dow and Monsanto and DuPont, on the other hand, seemed almost to relish the opportunity to decry a fellow corporation's misdeeds. They immediately expanded their production of the textiles, pigments, and pesticides that had been Sweeting-Aldren's mainstay—products for which demand in America only increased—and took the lead in demonizing Sweeting-Aldren's management. DuPont called the Peabody tragedy the work of "a bunch of devils." (DuPont's own managers were family men, not devils; they welcomed the EPA's intelligent regulation.) Monsanto solemnly swore that it had never employed injection wells and never would. Dow took pride in its foresight in locating its plants in one of the most geologically stable places in the world. By August sales and stock prices were up at all three companies.

In the public imagination "Sweeting-Aldren" joined the ranks of "Saddam Hussein" and "Manuel Noriega" and "the Medellín cartel." These were the guys with hats as black as the tabloid headlines screaming of their villainy, the men who made the good world bad. The United States bore the responsibility for punishing them, and if they couldn't be punished, the United States bore the responsibility for cleaning up after them; and if the clean-up proved painfully expensive, it could be argued that the United States bore the responsibility for having allowed them to become villains in the first place. But in no case did the American people themselves feel responsible.

As the weeks went by, out-of-town visitors occasionally ventured north from Boston to see the fences around Zone I. They had seen these fences countless times on television, and still it amazed them that Peabody could be reached by car in half an hour—that this land belonged to the earth as surely as the land in their own hometowns, that the weather and light didn't change as they approached the fences. They took photographs that, developed back in Los Angeles or Kansas City, showed a scene they again could not believe was real.

Bostonians, meanwhile, had more important things to think about. Low-interest federal loans had reignited the local economy. The window frames of downtown buildings had again been filled with unbroken greenish glass. Fenway Park had passed its safety inspections. And the Red Sox were still in first place.

THE CHILDREN OF ISAN

ISAN

CHARUNEE NORMITA THONGTHAM

Charunee Normita Thongtham was born in San Jose City, the Philippines. She taught for one year at the College of the Republic in the Philippines and in 1969 moved to Thailand. In 1977 she joined the staff of the *Bangkok Post*, where she has worked both as an environmental columnist and an editor. She is currently a features editor.

Ms. Thongtham received the Global 500 Award from the United Nations Environmental Program for her coverage of environmental issues. Her articles have been published in England, Germany, and Sweden.

Ms. Thongtham and her husband, M. L. Charuphant Thongtham, live in Bangkok. They have two children, Nalinee and Asawin.

Hua Lamphong Railway Station in Bangkok is a bee-
hive of activity at all hours of the day and night. Migrant
workers from the northeastern province of Isan arrive
in groups, and those working in Bangkok go home for a
visit. Bags in hand, new arrivals who have no jobs waiting
for them seek out the assistance of employment agencies
around the station.

On the several occasions that this writer went to the
station to observe the noisy comings and goings, I was
accosted by young men from the agencies asking whether
I was looking for a helper. "What do you prefer, a girl
or a boy? How much are you willing to pay as monthly
salary?" they asked. For all they knew, I could have been
a brothel owner. As long as they received their commission, they couldn't have cared less.

Forced by nature to leave their villages to find work
elsewhere, most of the people of the Northeast are hard-
working and honest. The increasing incidence of drought
in the region has driven able-bodied inhabitants to seek
employment in Bangkok and elsewhere.

Comprising seventeen provinces and one third of
Thailand's total land mass, the Northeast, popularly
known as Isan, is Thailand's largest region. Its agricultural land accounts for more than 40 percent of the
national total, but its population, predominantly rice
and tapioca farmers, earn the lowest per capita income
in the country because of poor soil and erratic rainfall.

There are two schools of thought as to why the Northeast is so poor agriculturally. One theory blames it on
the geological features of the region. The soil is sandy
and can hardly store water, which is why the region is
totally dry in the summer despite the fact that its total
rainfall is greater than that of agriculturally richer northern
Thailand. If that were not enough, Isan occupies the Korat

plateau, which sits on a big block of salt. Construction of dams and irrigation canals would raise the groundwater and, along with it, the salt, leading to salinization of farmland.

The other school of thought blames Isan's plight on the deforestation that has altered the country's overall rainfall pattern. According to Forestry Department statistics, 66 percent of Thailand's land area—about 320,697 square miles—was covered by forests in the 1950s. By 1973 forest cover was down to 43 percent. By the beginning of 1989 only 28.03 percent of forest cover remained.

That latest figure of 28.03 percent was the result of a survey made by a Landsat satellite of *all* areas with trees— forest reserves, national parks, and mangroves—except rubber plantations and so may have included tropical fruit plantations. If so, actual forest cover is significantly less than that cited.

Thai environmentalists claim that Thailand has only 10 to 15 percent of its forested land left. One Thai academic insists there is even less. "There are so many conflicting reports on how much forest Thailand has," said Uthit Kudin, associate professor at the Kasetsart University Faculty of Forestry and head of its Forest Biology Department. "But the truth is that Thailand now has only six percent of virgin forest left." He explained that although 12 percent of the forest cover has been set aside as forest reserves, national parks, and wildlife sanctuaries, most represents small islands of greenery with villagers living around them, and all have seen human activity.

In the Northeast especially, only small pockets of forests remain to serve the villages as sources of wood for housing and fuel, food and medicine. In the space of only one generation, just 24 years, the region's forest cover dwindled from 42 percent in 1961 to 13 percent in 1985 as the villagers cleared forests to gain farmland. This was largely the result of an increasing population and a corresponding rise in demand for agricultural land.

Once trees have been cleared, it takes only a few years for the thin soil on the denuded mountain slopes to erode away, but the effects of the destruction of watersheds last for generations: Poverty, infertile soil, and prolonged drought have been the lot of the Isan people from one generation to the next. Whether because of its geographical features, deforestation, or a combination of the two, one thing is sure: Drought has become an annual phenomenon in Isan, and with the drought a new pattern of internal migration has emerged.

In July farmers plant rice, a staple in Thailand. By January the wind brings waves of heat, and the rice fields, ponds, and marshes begin to dry up. Most young village men and women disappear, one by one or in small groups, to seek employment elsewhere. In the poorest villages of Roi Et, Maha Sarakham, and Buri Ram provinces only the young and the old are left behind, with grandparents looking after their grandchildren as the children's parents join the exodus of migrant workers to Bangkok and other provinces.

"It has become the custom for Isan children to come to Bangkok as soon as they finish sixth grade," says Amporn Suphananond, a housemaid from a remote village in Ubon Ratchathani. "I was already 17 when I left my village to come to Bangkok 14 years ago, but younger generations can hardly wait until they are old enough. My nieces and the other children in our neighborhood came to seek employment in the city as soon as they turned 13."

With no money to continue their education, the majority of farmers' children leave school after finishing sixth grade to help their parents plant rice or look after the family buffaloes. But with droughts nearly every year, the rice fields have become too dry to plant much of anything. The harvest is often very limited or virtually nonexistent.

"Most [rural children] are compelled by poverty to leave, to find work elsewhere and then send their earnings to support their families back home," says Amporn, herself the only breadwinner for her aging mother and a mentally ill elder sister. "For rural children, Bangkok is the legendary pot of gold at the end of the rainbow."

As a live-in maid for a family of four, Amporn cooks, does the laundry, cleans the house, sweeps the yard, waters plants, and feeds her employers' menagerie of pets, all for 1,800 baht, or around $70, a month. Despite the small pay she considers herself lucky, for at least she eats three meals a day and, more important, she is able to support her mother and sister.

Before she came to Bangkok to work, fifty cents went a long way for Porn and her family. "Money was difficult to earn, so we were reluctant to spend any money we had unless it was really necessary. We would collect bamboo shoots to eat with fermented fish or would dig for insects, snails, and frogs in the fields; but even those are now becoming rare because of prolonged droughts and the increase in population." Amporn's two nieces also came to Bangkok and found work through an agent. One of them, Amornrat, had to work without pay for two months in return for the fee that her employer paid the agent.

Amornrat was employed by a noodle shop, where she worked as a waitress, dishwasher, and janitor all rolled into one for 300 baht, or less than $12, a month. She did not have her own room; after the shop had closed at night she had to clear some of the tables for a place to sleep, only to get up early the next morning to go to the market and then help prepare the food and put the shop in order before it opened for business at 10 in the morning.

It was a heavy job for a 13-year-old, and Amornrat lasted only a few months. She had to go home anyway; the rainy season had started and her father wrote that he could do with an extra hand in the rice fields, as her brothers were too young to help.

In Bangkok finding a live-in maid is not difficult. What is difficult is finding someone who will stay the entire year without taking a leave. Most maids go home during the rainy season to help their families plant the fields, and then later in the year to help with the harvest. "If the youngsters did not go home to give a helping hand, their parents wouldn't be able to finish the rice planting before the rainy season ended," Amporn explains.

After the rice-planting season, the exodus back to Bangkok resumes.

Amornrat says that each year agents from Bangkok go to the villages to recruit 13-year-old children fresh from school. Promising the parents that they will look after the children well, they pay the children's train fare to Bangkok and find work for them. They then collect two to three months' wages in advance from the employers, and the children have to work without pay until they have paid off the fee.

Many children are sold to sweatshops and forced to work from dawn to late at night in small factories. A girl of 14 who was rescued by police from a Chinese family-owned candy factory told how she and other children were made to work for 12 to 14 hours a day, seven days a week, wrapping candies. Food consisted of rice gruel with some vegetables, and at night the children slept side by side on the floor of a crowded, poorly ventilated room. They were given only a pittance for their labor; the employer claimed that their wages had been taken in advance by the agent, who said the money was badly needed by the impoverished parents back home. When they were discovered, the children all evidenced signs of malnutrition.

The candy factory is not an isolated case, as ignorant

and desperate parents allow their children to be taken away and exploited by strangers promising to find them work in the city. Factories employing child labor are often surrounded by high walls, and the living quarters have iron bars on the windows; hence escape is out of the question. Besides, without money and unfamiliar with Bangkok, the children are afraid to escape.

But a worse fate awaits some unwary teenagers seeking fortune in the city. The fathers of two youngsters recently sued a Bangkok food shop owner, accusing him of sexual and physical abuse and forced confinement of their children. Miak Pew-on, a farmer in Isan, told the Civil Court that Suvit Namsawangnet hired his 13-year-old daughter as a helper on January 1, 1991.

"Since then she has been constantly tortured and sexually assaulted," he claimed.

Another Isan farmer, Riam Changlek, 57, said similar physical and sexual assault was inflicted on his 16-year-old son who was hired by the shop owner to work as a kitchen hand. Both fathers were suing for damages.

Some girls are told they have been hired as waitresses, only to find themselves in brothels. Unwilling girls are imprisoned in heavily guarded rooms until they are sold to customers and lose their virginity. Those who resist are tortured and chained until they submit.

A few years ago a fire broke out in a brothel in Phuket, southern Thailand. Later the charred bodies of five young girls with heavy chains around their ankles were found among the ashes. Investigation revealed that the girls were from Isan; one grieving mother told police that her 17-year-old daughter had left home with a friend three months earlier to find work in Bangkok. She had promised to send money to support the family, but they had not heard from her since.

Some prostitution ring victims do try to escape, to no avail. Others, feeling dirty and having nothing more to lose, become resigned to their fate, taking consolation in the fact that, although the brothel owner takes a big cut from their earnings, they still earn more than a housemaid and thus are able to support their family better. Others have actually managed to buy farmland for their landless parents, pay off their debts or build a new house for them, and send their younger brothers and sisters to school.

Providing cheap labor as housemaids, baby-sitters, gardeners, gasoline boys, factory workers, road workers, and building construction workers, the people of Isan have contributed much to Bangkok's economic and infrastructural development. The more enterprising become taxi or *tuk-tuk* (tricycle) drivers and food vendors hawking Isan food to their fellow Northeasterners at construction sites.

As multistory hotels, department stores, condominiums, and office buildings rise, men as well as women and children from Isan can be seen standing precariously on scaffoldings doing masonry, carrying bricks, mixing sand with cement, and doing other manual labor, all for a daily wage of 70 baht ($2.75) for women and children 13 years old and above, and 100 baht ($3.92) for men.

"It is better than nothing," says Ponsri Sricharoen, 40, of Nong Khai. "After the rice-planting season we might as well come to Bangkok to work in construction and earn some money rather than just wait for harvest time. Come harvest season, we take leave and go home."

She is luckier than most, because her eight hectares of rice paddies are well irrigated by water from the Mekong River, which separates Thailand and Laos. But with no one to look after their son, she and her husband bring him with them.

Needless to say, the children of construction workers have no opportunity to go to school, as their parents move from one project to another. During the day the children play among themselves at the construction site; at night they and their parents retire to makeshift huts of wood and corrugated iron in a corner of the work site.

When the children are old enough to carry bricks or remove leftover pieces of wood, they also work to augment the family income. Ponsri's son is only 13, and he is proud that he earns as much as his mother. But he started at only 40 baht, or $1.56, per day when he was 11.

Not all migrant workers have land back home. Some have sold their land to pay off debts, and with no reason to go back they make Bangkok their permanent home. Others, like the taxi and the *tuk-tuk* drivers, fetch their wives and children once they are established so that the family can be together again.

The growth of Bangkok's population, from one million in 1953 to seven million today, owing in large part to migration from rural areas, has led to housing problems and the need for more schools, hospitals, and clean drinking water as well as a solid-waste disposal system, transport facilities, and public utilities.

Bangkok has not been capable of meeting these needs to the full. Slums continue to grow, there is a shortage of hospital beds, public buses are always crowded, and to date the municipality does not have even one waste-water treatment plant. Bangkok was once called the Venice of the East for the many canals that crisscross the city, but most canals have been filled in and turned into roads, and the few that remain are so polluted that pedestrians cover their noses with handkerchiefs when walking past them.

Even the Chao Phraya River, or River of Kings, which is featured in many tourist brochures and has served as an important means of communication since the founding of Bangkok more than 200 years ago, is heavily polluted. And no wonder, for all of the city's sewage, not to mention industrial wastes and runoff of agricultural chemicals, winds up in the river. In the summer when the water is low the oxygen content in the lower part of the Chao Phraya is almost nil, according to tests conducted by the Thai National Environment Board (NEB).

Bangkok's air is also heavily polluted, not so much from industry as from vehicle emissions. The NEB's monitoring data on air quality rated the capital's atmosphere as "dangerous" throughout 1989, with the average quality index reaching 277, nearly three times the maximum acceptable level of 100.

Air pollution in the city was even worse in 1990. Speculators made money on the stock exchange, and a concomitant increase in land value and building construction created an overnight economic boom that turned many small landowners into multimillionaires. Even office clerks and company drivers became real estate agents in their spare time, and as they made money they bought cars. More cars meant more air pollution. The Thai government imposed limits on the sale and use of unleaded gasoline in May 1991, but that has not reduced Bangkok's air pollution.

Based on the present rate of increase, the NEB estimates that by the year 2000 Bangkok will have nearly three million vehicles whereas the number of roads will remain almost the same. That, of course, would lead to more traffic congestion, Bangkok's chronic problem for the past 10 years, which reached a critical stage in 1990.

Even as Bangkok struggles with the environmental problems created by its burgeoning population, environmental refugees pour in from the Northeast and elsewhere, hoping to find the imaginary pot of gold at the end of the rainbow.

October 31, 1989. A tropical depression in the South China Sea was reported to be headed south toward the

Gulf of Thailand. As it advanced, it rapidly developed into a tropical storm.

Over the next three days the storm took on the more threatening character of a typhoon and again changed direction, this time moving north. On November 4, Typhoon Gay, with winds of 75 miles per hour at its center, slammed into the coast of Chumphon, 289 miles south of Bangkok.

For eight hours the typhoon vented its fury on Chumphon, flattening houses in four districts, killing 529 people, rendering 32,301 families homeless, and wiping out 142,402 hectares of coconut and rubber plantations and fruit orchards. Another 1,517 fishermen were lost at sea, their bodies never found.

Many of those who died in Chumphon were migrant workers from Isan who did manual labor on rubber plantations or worked on fishing boats.

Apart from funeral expenses of 5,000 baht ($200) per family from the Thai Department of Fisheries, the surviving family members of migrant workers from the Northeastern provinces, approximately 8,000 people, received no relief from the government. To receive assistance, typhoon victims had to present their house registrations—proof that they were registered residents of Chumphon, which the visiting Northeasterners did not have.

Perhaps there is hope that such disasters can be prevented in the future. Before Typhoon Gay devastated Chumphon, most Thais did not know what a typhoon was. How they ask: Was the typhoon the result of the felling of trees? Is it comparable to events in two other southern provinces, where deforestation of mountains caused mudslides and floods that killed hundreds of people and rendered thousands homeless in 1988?

As Thailand's overall rainfall pattern becomes erratic and the droughts worsen, Thais are relearning the value of trees. With help from the Thai Army, projects have been initiated to make Isan green again, and villagers in the Northeast have started to protect their forests.

FIELDS OF BALM

J. B. McCOURTNEY

J.B. McCourtney, at left

J. B. McCourtney was born in Sarasota, Florida. He studied at Exeter College of Art in Devon and at Medway College of Design in Rochester, Kent, England. His photographic documentary pursuits have taken him to Europe, North Africa, Brazil, and the farms of Florida. He is currently working on a project documenting social transitions in southwest Florida.

Mr. McCourtney lives in Florida with his wife, Sandra, and five children.

O n November 15, 1989, what the Environmental Protection Agency (EPA) has called "the nation's worst mass pesticide poisoning" occurred at Goodson Farms in Balm, Florida. Eighty-five farm workers absorbed the pesticide mevinphos through their skin. Commonly known by the brand name Phosdrin, the pesticide had done to humans what it was designed to do to insects: attack the nervous system. Symptoms of exposure to this highly toxic pesticide included vomiting, convulsions, and loss of consciousness. "I was cutting cauliflower about 10 in the morning, when I felt dizzy and started throwing up," explained José Luiz Rodriguez, a cauliflower cutter. "Workers were carrying other workers who were falling to the ground." The poisoned workers went to the Ruskin Migrant Health Center, where Dr. Dennis Penzell and his staff were the first to treat them. Twelve pesticide victims were then admitted to intensive care units in local hospitals. "I went back to my trailer; I did not go to the hospital," Rodriguez said. "[Goodson] pressured me into returning to work the next day, where they gave me a yellow raincoat and boots." Others lost their jobs because they could not return to work for several days.

"We were all shaking, sweating, dizzy, and vomiting. Two months later I still had headaches," recalled José "Chepe" Mendoza, a crew chief responsible for 26 of the workers. "Goodson asked me to bring my people back to work. I told my boss, 'My people are sick, they can't work.' After three or four weeks I was told, 'Mendoza, we don't need you now. Come back tomorrow.' Every day after, it was, 'Come back tomorrow.'"

In west central Florida some 40,000 migratory farm workers harvest a large range of crops. This farming district extends 50 miles from the fields of Dover and Wimauma in the north to the celery fields of Sarasota County in the south. Here, farming communities are segregated from mainstream society by poverty and culture and are without formal union representation. Thus the farm workers' situation is ripe for abuses.

The workers' environment is totally contaminated by pesticides. Their camps and trailer homes are surrounded by fields where the ground has been chemically saturated year after year. Workers must wear protective clothing in the field, worry about the water they drink, and seek medical care frequently.

Of the eight fields this journalist entered, two were being sprayed while workers were picking. On most occasions I experienced burning sensations on my exposed skin. Few workers complain for fear of job loss, and at least one Goodson Farm worker, Juana Lucia Galvan, views the management benignly: "Goodson has always protected us; we are the ones that don't obey." She adds: "I am not afraid of chemicals."

The harvesting schedule is dictated both by crop conditions and by local market trends. The Goodson Farms pesticide incident, in the fields of Balm, occurred when harvesting workers were sent into a sprayed field before the 48-hour waiting period, mandated for reentry into a Phosdrin-treated field, had elapsed.

Goodson Farms was charged with seven violations of Florida state law and fined $7,000, and its privilege of using Phosdrin and other extremely toxic, restricted-use pesticides was revoked for sixteen months. However, the incident prompted the Florida House of Representatives to review the state's 16-year-old pesticide law. In May 1990 the House passed a bill that increased penalties from a maximum of $1,000 per violation to $10,000 per violation. Meanwhile, the need for improved enforcement is apparent. There are currently only 11 full-time state pesticide inspectors to protect the rights of Florida's 200,000 migrant farm workers.

The agriculture industry, under the joint jurisdiction of the Occupational Safety and Health Administration and the Department of Labor, is the only American industry in which children comprise a significant part of the work-force.

On both state and national levels, farm worker advocates are highly concerned about the long-term effects of working, living, and socializing in a toxic environment. Dr. Marion Moses is an EPA advisor and the nation's leading authority on pesticide-related illness among farm workers. Discussing the workers, she recalls the practice of carrying canaries into coal mines to test for the presence of toxic gases. The country's 2.5 million migratory farm workers, Dr. Moses says, have become "canaries for the consumer."

Warning sign at the gate of an orange grove, Wimauma, Florida.

Before planting, the ground is injected with the potent pesticide methyl bromide, sterilizing the entire area.

Tractor/sprayer spraying pesticides in a celery field (detail).

Celery cutter working by piece rate.

On average, vegetable crops are sprayed every five or six days and for persistent pests more often, as in the case of these bell peppers.

Pesticide labels stipulate washing hands after contact, particularly before eating. In the field, there is no running water. Workers on break, Wimauma, Florida.

Farm labor camps house the workers' families. The fenced camps adjoin the fields and are locked in the evenings.

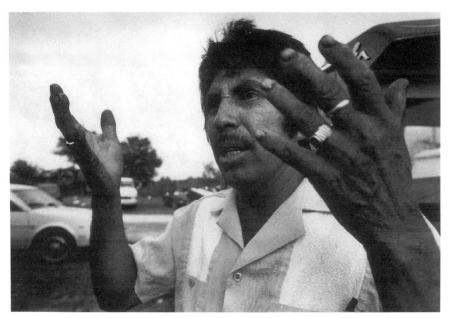

José "Chepe" Mendoza, crew chief at Goodson Farms, Balm, Florida.

Tomato pickers with crew chief atop truck, Wimauma, Florida.

A tractor mixing station where constant pesticide runoff contaminates area fields and irrigation ditches.

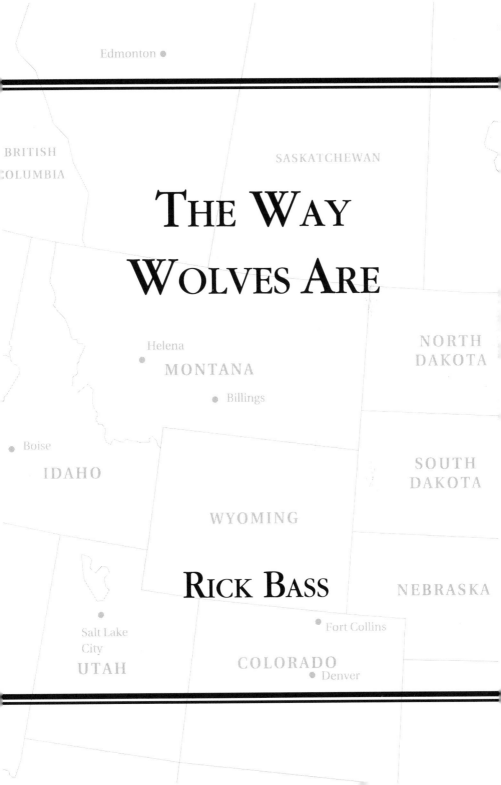

THE WAY
WOLVES ARE

RICK BASS

Rick Bass was born in Fort Worth, Texas. He studied geology and wildlife science at Utah State University and has worked as a biologist in Arkansas and a geologist in Mississippi. He is the author of *The Watch*, a collection of short stories, and four collections of essays, *The Deer Pasture; Wild to the Heart; Oil Notes;* and most recently, *Winter*. His work has appeared in a number of prize-winning anthologies.

Mr. Bass currently lives in Montana with his wife, Elizabeth.

In 1892, Francis Parkman wrote eloquently about how even then America's big predators (other than man) were disappearing.

". . . Those discordant serenaders, the wolves that howled at evening about the traveller's camp-fire, have succumbed to arsenic and hushed their savage music. . . . The mountain lion shrinks from the face of man, and even grim 'Old Ephraim,' the grizzly bear, seeks the seclusion of his dens and caverns."

Because we could not take time to manage our livestock effectively, wolf depredation upon free-ranging sheep and cattle was a significant hardship on ranchers before and during the turn of the century. Rather than trying to change management practices and strike a balance between the land and themselves, ranchers instead eradicated wolves completely, with the government's aid. The last known wolf pack to den in Montana was in the 1930s. They were gone for sixty years, but now they're coming back. Biologists believe that Montana's large deer herds are "luring" them back.

Public support is largely in favor of the wolves' return—two thirds of the general population and up to 90 percent of visitors to national parks want wolves back in the United States. A balance must be struck this time, however, and that balance should be based on a human understanding of wolves: their biology, sociology, and history. In the century before—and in all of our centuries before that one—we have rarely taken time to pay attention to the wolf itself. Myths and misconceptions have surrounded the animal over the ages.

Wolves eat about nine pounds of meat a day. A typical pack of six wolves in Montana kill a deer or elk about once a week. They like to hunt at night and sleep in the day. Only one pair from each pack mate, once a year—the alpha male (the dominant male in the pack) and the alpha female. They have a long courtship that sometimes begins in the late fall and intensifies in January, and the pair then breed in late January or early February. Gestation is sixty-three days—the same as for dogs. The pups, usually numbering six, are born in April. The pack spend the summer taking care of the pups. "Aunts" baby-sit the young wolves whenever the alpha female leaves the den. By the fall the pups have grown so much that they are indistinguishable from the adults. They're ready to learn to hunt.

Wolves are loyal to both their pack and their mate; sometimes they mate for life. Stanley Young, a biologist in the Southwest, tells of trapping a male Mexican wolf; the wolf's mate returned to the capture site for sixteen nights in a row, until she too was caught. John Murray, a writer in Alaska, tells the story of a pregnant alpha female in Denali National Park who strayed too far from her den. She had to stop on her way back and give birth out on the tundra, in a small depression out of the wind. It was twenty-four hours before she could move the pups, so the rest of the pack brought her snowshoe hares and stood guard to protect her and the newborn pups from any prowling grizzlies.

Wolves are full of passion and mystery. Mythology tells us that pricking oneself with a sharpened wolf's breastbone can stave off death. Native Americans say that wolves' howls are the cries of lost spirits trying to make it back to earth.

For sure, they're making it back to Montana. It is estimated that Montana now has between forty and sixty wolves. Some of those wolves may even make it down to Yellowstone, where wolves have been absent for almost seventy years. A famous Russian proverb says that "The wolf is kept fed by his feet." A wolf in Scandanavia, pursued by dogs and hunters, traveled 125 miles in twenty-four hours. Young "disperser" wolves often leave their pack when they are unable to gain an alpha ranking and go off on their own, looking for new territories. It is conceivable that wolves could return to Yellowstone in this manner. The park has an overabundance of deer and elk—one of the highest concentrations in the world—and it is thought that the wolf would provide a good selective pressure on the burgeoning herds.

Wolves are *loaded* with passion. Two years ago a wolf pack in Alaska hunted down and killed three grizzly bears because the grizzlies had wandered too close to their den while they had pups in the den: a show of disrespect on the grizzlies' part. Normally grizzlies dominate wolves—they run them off of a wolf-killed carcass and claim the spoils, draping themselves across the kill—and grizzlies even eat wolves when they can catch and kill them.

This time it wasn't about food. It was about territorial defense, and anger. Seven wolves went out the next day and killed those three grizzlies in what biologists can only explain as an unprecedented display of revenge.

Wolves also fight to keep their territories free of other canids—coyotes, dogs, and even other wolf packs. They scent-mark the boundaries of their territories with urine, making circuits every few days to keep them well established. Sometimes prey species such as deer and elk learn that adjacent wolf packs do not like to "test" each other's borders, so the deer or elk hang out along the "no-man's land" between the two territories, often a geographical feature such as a high wooded ridge or a river bottom.

There are romantic histories in the West of lonely wolves taking up a friendship with someone's pet dog—especially around the time when the wolves were being killed off—but more frequently wolves hate dogs.

Again, there seems to be at times—especially in August—an excess of passion. Steve Fritts and Bill Paul studied the interaction of wolves and dogs in Minnesota and wrote, "Several breeds of dogs were killed, ranging in size from a miniature poodle to a Norwegian elkhound. Based on our investigations and interviews with dog owners, we believe that small- to medium-sized dogs, which may be particularly excitable and vocal, are more likely to provoke attack by wolves.

". . . While preying on dogs, wolves displayed a lack of fear of humans and buildings that is otherwise unknown except when they are diseased, disabled, or preying on deer. In several incidents investigated, wolves evidently focused their attention on dogs so intently that they were almost oblivious to buildings and humans . . . In one case, a wolf attacked a dog near the doorstep and wouldn't retreat until beaten with a shovel."

The tendency at this stage of discovery of the way wolves are is to counter such a "bad" image with a "good" one—to tell about the male wolf in Montana last year who, after the female was shot, raised their six pups by himself. But this judgment, this notion of good and bad, is what led to the imbalance and misunderstanding between wolves and humans in the first place. *It's just the way they are.* We need to make up our minds this time whether or not we can live with it.

The romantic mind might note that sixty-plus years—the length of the wolves' absence—is how long it would take for ninety-nine percent of the old-time Indian-killers, buffalo-killers, and wolf-killers to die off: as if the wolves could not bring themselves to return to a country where such wanton killers still ruled.

There is no other word for our behavior back then.

The easiest way to kill wolves then (and now) was with poison, and it was used from Mexico up through Texas and all the way across the West and up into the Arctic. Joseph Taylor wrote in his 1891 book *Twenty Years on the Trap Line* that "poisoned wolves and foxes in their dying fits often slobber upon the grass, which becoming sun dried holds its poisonous properties a long time, often causing the death months or even years after of the pony, antelope, buffalo, or animals feeding upon it. The Indians losing their stock in this way feel like making reprisals, and often did."

Bully for them. Young tells in his book *The Last of the Loners* how buffalo hunters and wolf trappers in Kansas in the 1870s had paved a road with wolf bones. The torturing and maiming of wolves is recounted in stunning detail in Barry Lopez's book, *Of Wolves and Men*; setting live wolves on fire is the one that troubles me the most.

Torture seems to have been a cultural phenomenon that, with the exception of poisoning, has vanished. Poisoning continues with vigor in both Canada and Mexico and is one reason the Mexican wolf—there may be only a dozen left in the wild—has been unable to re-populate the southwestern United States.

In the 1860s three "wolf-getters" took more than three thousand wolves, coyotes, and foxes with poison in a single year. The entire kill netted them $2,500. Song-birds—larks—were killed for bait, laced with strychnine, and then scattered like candy along known wolf runways.

It became an unwritten rule of the range for ranchers to carry poison in their saddlebags and never pass up a carcass of any kind without injecting it with strychnine.

"They would kill a buffalo and cut the meat in small pieces," William E. Webb wrote in 1872, "which were scattered in all directions, a half mile or so from camp, and so bait the wolves for about two days. . . . Mean-while all hands were preparing meat in pieces about 2" square . . . putting a quantity of strychnine in the center. One morning after putting out the poison they picked up sixty-four wolves, and none of them over a mile and a half from camp."

Sixty-four wolves in a morning? (The pack sizes were

larger then, out on the plains, to bring down buffalo from the great herds. That size of wolf pack will never be seen again, unless the buffalo herds return.)

I picture a mile-wide circle of dying wolves, the prairie *writhing* with them in the moonlight as they flopped and backflipped in their slow deaths . . .

The primary prey of wolves in northwestern Montana is white-tailed deer. Wolves are such social animals that they rarely kill or eat anything that they have not seen other pack members—their family—kill and eat.

Occasionally, however, a wolf, or wolves, kill livestock. They are not nearly as great a predator of sheep and cows as are coyotes; if ranchers would stop and think about it, they might realize that wolves are one of the easiest biological ways to suppress coyote populations. The ranchers' argument that wolves are a financial burden to them no longer holds water: For the last few years a private organization, the Defenders of Wildlife, has been reimbursing ranchers 100 percent for each confirmed wolf predation of ranchers' livestock. (Defenders does not reimburse for coyote depredations.)

The ranchers say they are responding to the economics of the situation, but what they are really responding to is history and a deep, old cultural tradition of wolf-hating that will be hard to change. Despite the complete reimbursement by Defenders of Wildlife, and despite the fact that the wolf is (theoretically) protected under the Endangered Species Act, some ranchers in Montana are still shooting wolves. At least five have been shot in the last two years. Sometimes the ranchers call the authorities (the U.S. Fish and Wildlife Service or Animal Damage Control) to come and get the carcass, despite the penalty for killing a wolf of a $100,000 fine and a year in jail. (No charges have ever been pressed.)

This is not to say that all ranchers these days are wolf-killers. For every wolf-hating rancher, there seems to be one who is willing to let things sort themselves out, to give the wolves a chance.

What the wolf-hating ranchers are remembering are the old trap-crippled renegades who took to preying on the huge herds of cattle moving across the federal lands after the buffalo had all been killed off.

Wolf watchers in Montana these days tend to give the wolves names like "Puppy" and "Papa Wolf," but during the wolves' first incarnation in this country they had names like "The Black Devil" and "Bigfoot, the Terror of Lane County."

"Old Lefty of Burns Hole," in Colorado, was trapped by the left foot in 1913. Lefty succeeded, writes Stanley Young, "in twisting off the better part of his left foot from the trap . . . and then making its escape. As a result of its missing front foot, the stub of which completely healed in time, it had adopted a very peculiar gait. It never put the stub of its left foot to the ground . . . In eight years, Old Lefty was credited with the killing of 384 head of livestock."

The Syca Wolf of southern Oregon, an old male with greatly worn teeth, was credited with killing many horses and cattle. Three Toes of Harding County (South Dakota) had $50,000 worth of killings attributed to him. The Queen Wolf—also called the Unaweep Wolf—wreaked significant havoc in the early 1920s and had a malformed foot caused by a trap injury.

In reading a history of the "famous" wolves of the West, a picture emerges that does not grant the wolf total absolution from cow-killing, but one that has rarely been commented upon: the preponderance of injuries that seems to turn wolves toward easier prey.

The Ghost Wolf of the Judith Basin, which killed $35,000 worth of livestock in Montana in the 1920s and early 1930s, seemed to turn pathologic, often just wounding livestock.

The Ghost Wolf had been shot in the hind leg and knocked down but escaped capture by hiding in a snowdrift. Ranchers tried to run it down in their cars. Once five Russian wolfhounds cornered and attacked it, battling for hours, but it got away when, writes Bert Lindler, "the wolf escaped up a steep mountainside, with the man, horse and dogs too tired to follow."

Sixty-five traps and poison baits were set out for the Ghost Wolf at one time, to no avail. Lindler interviewed Ed Kolar, eighty years old, about his memories of the Ghost Wolf.

"He [Kolar] remembers when the wolf killed a short yearling," Lindler writes. "'The cow came home with the whole rear end torn out of her,' Kolar said. 'We had to kill her.'"

The Ghost Wolf was also called the White Wolf. Trappers stayed in the area for five and six months at a time, laying out poison balls and baits, killing everything but the White Wolf.

"On May 8, 1930," Lindler writes, "Earl Neill and Al E. Close tracked the Ghost Wolf from Close's ranch into Pig Eye Basin in the Little Belt Mountains. They were aided by a German shepherd and an Irish terrier they had trained that winter hunting coyotes.

"The dogs jumped the Ghost Wolf, who fought them. They kept pushing the wolf toward Close, who was hiding behind a tree. When the wolf was forty yards away, Close stepped out.

"'And do you know, I almost didn't shoot,' Close said. 'It was the hardest thing I think I did. There was a perfect shot, the grandest old devil . . . I thought swiftly that these were the hills over which he had hunted. I knew that it was the cruel nature of the wilderness—the fight for the survival of the fittest—that made him the ferocious hunter that he was . . .

"'. . . Luckily I came to my senses in time and let the bullet fly fairly into the face of the old criminal.'"

So far in Montana, in their present reincarnation, there haven't been any terrible devil-wolves. One wolf killed four lambs. A pack of four wolves killed two steers but ate only twenty pounds of the meat before turning away. Would they have killed again? We can't say for sure; they were shot with tranquilizers from a helicopter (one escaped) and relocated in a more northern part of the state, where two of them were then shot, while the third one got into those four lambs . . .

Wolf recovery in Montana cannot succeed without the ranchers helping in the new balance. It is a matter of understanding that some livestock—but probably not much—will be lost but will be paid for by people who love the wolf, such as Defenders of Wildlife.

Wolves *prefer* wild game; that's proven. Wolves' depredation on livestock in extreme northern Minnesota—the only place in the lower forty-eight where wolves are not listed as endangered species (they're given a "threatened" status in Minnesota)—affects less than one percent of the ranches.

Similarly, in Manitoba livestock remains were found in only one percent of all the scats collected in a national park, despite the fact that the park is surrounded by farmland and cattle.

In Montana coyotes sometimes kill between three and seven cows per year out of an individual herd. Wolves have killed only sixteen cows over the last four years; that averages about one cow per year out of every twenty thousand available.

Under the federal wolf recovery plan, a wolf is given two chances these days. It is relocated to a new area following livestock depredation (if it can be trapped or darted; otherwise it is killed); if depredation occurs a second time, the wolf is killed or captured and put in captivity.

As wolves begin to regain public notice in Montana, ranchers sometimes attribute coyote-killed livestock to wolves. One rancher reported losing a 250-pound calf to wolves this summer and called federal authorities, who discovered that the calf had died from an ulcerated rumen, not predation. The rancher agreed with the analysis and felt bad about having called the authorities out on Father's Day.

Steve Fritts, a federal biologist in Montana who studied wolf depredations on livestock in Minnesota, writes that "it seems that depredations at some farms may stop even though few or no wolves are removed; at other farms depredations continue despite wolves being captured regularly."

Healthy wolves prefer to live in the woods and hunt wild game, shunning contact with humans and their livestock. The Russians have a proverb concerning the wolves they would catch as pups and try to turn into pets: "You may feed the wolf as much as you like, he will always glance toward the forest." Wolf studies indicate that when winters are hard and the snows are deep wolves prey even more regularly on wild animals than on that one percent of domestic livestock, because the deep snow favors the wolves during a chase; their huge snowshoe paws don't allow them to flounder and sink through the snow the way the hooved animals do: deer, elk, and moose.

But all these wonderful statistics are only that: numbers. Wolves *will* kill cattle every now and then. (*Everything* will kill sheep, unless the sheep are watched constantly and carefully: coyotes, wild dogs, eagles, ravens, bears, even other sheep—they trample each other in a stunningly mindless fashion.) It is an unfair pressure to place upon the species to expect that all wolves will avoid all cattle all of the time.

The truth of the matter, however, is that wolves in the West will never be out of control again. The great buffalo herds are long gone, ancient ghosts, and with them the big wolf packs that followed them.

And I like to imagine, to *hope*, that a new culture is being formed: that as each year passes a little education and tolerance happens, that the ranchers become more used to the new balance that is trying to establish itself between wilderness and farmland—a balance that does not always (one percent of the time?) stop at an arbitrary fence line, a rusty barbed wire or buck-and-rail fence that will be gone anyway in thirty or forty years . . .

Barry Lopez writes of interviewing some old aerial hunters and trappers in Minnesota.

"The aerial hunter, trapping on the ground one year, caught a large male black wolf in one of his traps. As he approached, the wolf lifted his trapped foot, extended it toward him, and whined softly. 'I would have let him go if I didn't need the money awful bad,' he said gently."

The fact that some humans will always be mystified, even terrified, by wolves—the nearly unshakable depth of that knee-jerk reaction, the old culture—was made painfully clear to me one January, at a bar in Fairbanks, Alaska.

The winter-sadness that sometimes goes with that landscape, in that season, was starting to set in, and at our table there were hunters and nonhunters, some animal rights people, and just plain environmentalists.

That long late-night winter-depressed aura was hovering, coupled with the general rage environmentalists sometimes find themselves rousing to when they're together and talking—their life's battle becoming a common ground for discussion—stories of atrocity being traded;

laments. Breast-beating. None of it was making anyone feel better, but it all has to be said.

A friend who races sled dogs was sinking into the winter, trying to claw her way back up out of the winter's pull with her rage alone. She was talking about this guy she heard bragging in this same bar—some dentist from Anchorage talking to his friend from Seattle about the "sport" of aerial hunting—chasing wolves across the tundra and through the willows in a small plane and shooting at them from the plane; or sometimes running the wolves to near-exhaustion and then getting out and throwing on the snowshoes and hobbling the last hundred yards to where the wolves are backed up against a small bluff, panting, and shooting them in that manner, shooting all of them . . .

But this dentist and his friend from Seattle were talking about a flight where they'd never landed the plane.

According to their brags, my friend said, they had just cruised along behind the wolves, with full flaps down and the throttle cut way back, aiming into a heavy wind, riding right on the pack's back, just a few feet above it, following it, and gaining on it, and sinking lower and lower as the shooter leaned and labored out the window to get his gun into position . . .

My friend says the dentist was speaking with dumb awe as he bragged: that that was the hopelessness, the utter life's despair hopelessness of it, that the dentist had been *right there*, so *close*, and yet had not been able to grip life's simple mystery, that what he was doing was wrong, that he was breaking up a social bond, that he was signing the wolves' death warrant, the death warrant of our respect for our place on the earth, and for respect in all forms and fashions . . .

But the dentist was so *close* to understanding, my friend said. He had *almost* seen it, she said: just by the way he was talking, the awe in his voice, and his eyes—he had almost seen it.

"I was right there," the dentist was saying, speaking as if in a trance. "I tell you, Joe, it was like nothing I've ever seen or done—Joe, for a few seconds there we were right in with them, following right behind them—and the big leader looked back and for a minute, Joe, following along behind them like that, it was like *we* were one of the pack . . ."

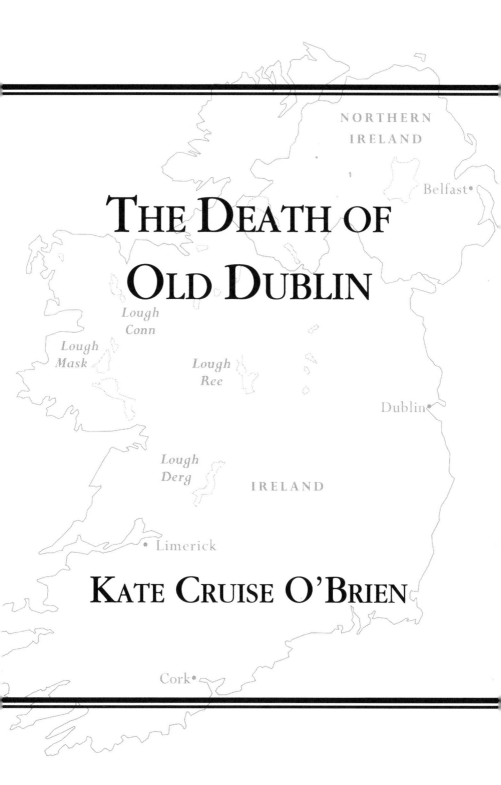

THE DEATH OF
OLD DUBLIN

KATE CRUISE O'BRIEN

Kate Cruise O'Brien was born in Dublin in 1948. She is a columnist for the *Irish Independent* and a teacher of creative writing. Ms. O'Brien is the author of two books, *A Gift Horse and Other Stories* and most recently *The Homesick Garden*, a novel. Her short stories have been published internationally. She was awarded both the Hennessy Award for New Irish Writing and the Rooney Prize for Irish Literature.

Ms. O'Brien's work has been featured in a number of newspapers and periodicals, including the *Sunday Correspondent*, *The Listener*, and the *Sunday Times of London*.

Ms. O'Brien lives in Dublin with her husband, Joseph Kearney, and son, Alexander.

1991 is Dublin's year as European City of Culture. Yes indeed. Goering once said that every time he heard the word culture he wanted to reach for his gun. I know Dublin people—most particularly people who care about the city—who feel the same way about our designation by the European Community as European cultural capital. There is nothing wrong with an honor, providing, of course, you deserve it. What is making some Dubliners feel queasy is the sense that we are wrapping robes around a skeleton. Now is not the time to honor Dublin or to feel complacent about it. Now is the time to try to save what is left of it.

In 1988 we held a "Millennium" year to celebrate a notional thousand years of Dublin. No one can be quite sure how old Dublin is, but that was felt to be beside the point. A celebration was ordered, so a celebration happened. The "Millennium" celebration did little to stop the destruction of Dublin. Since then we have destroyed the interiors of two fine churches. We have demolished early 18th-century houses with wood-paneled interiors on Bachelors Walk and Stephen's Green. We have lost the great stone wall of the former Bow Street distillery. A dual-carriage way is being driven through the oldest part of the city, destroying medieval street patterns. But never mind. They're planning to recreate "Old Dublin" as a theme park.

If I sound bitter and a bit confused about "we" and "they," then I am bitter and I am confused. Dubliners are continually being told by various PR people in Dublin Corporation—Dublin's city hall—that they can make a valuable contribution to the city's future. This makes us feel guilty when things, as they often do, go wrong. I didn't vote for an inner-city, dual-carriage way. I didn't want it. I was, however, quite powerless to stop it. Nobody in authority wanted to listen to my "valuable contribution." The voices of the thousands of people, like myself, who have tried to call a halt to the road plans that are destroying the city are voices crying in the wilderness. Frank McDonald, environment correspondent of *The Irish Times*, puts it better than I can. In an article entitled "City of Culture, how are yeh?" he wrote:

"They are just not listening, and it is now abundantly clear that we are beating our heads against a concrete wall. Is there any point in going on? Or has the time come, finally, for those of us who care about the survival of the city to throw in the towel?"

Grim stuff, highly emotional stuff, but Frank McDonald is not alone in his despair. I'm afraid that nobody has anything very good to say about dear old Dublin, Anna Livia, sweet, dirty hag, in this our celebratory year. In an article in the English *Independent* last year, Dan Cruickshank, a highly respected architectural historian, argued that no European city had done more, in recent years, to destroy its architectural heritage. Cruickshank talked of the "rape" of the city and reminded us, as if we needed reminding, that "Those who love Dublin and know it well fear that its current troubles could be terminal."

The problem is that those who need reminding aren't listening and those who don't need reminding are despairing.

I am one of those people who know Dublin and know it well. It's more than know. I love Dublin. I was born here, brought up here. This city has always conferred on me a unique feeling of excitement and safety. Now I am beginning to wonder, as Frank McDonald does, "Is there any point in going on?" Is there any point in continuing to care about something that is going to be destroyed? When do you stop beating your head against a concrete wall?

Who are "they," you must be wondering. Why is

Dublin being raped and/or destroyed? What is this concrete wall? Why should anyone talk about a city as if it were a dear friend or relation who needed an urgent life-saving operation?

Complicated questions those, but not impossible to answer. I shall tell it, as far as I can, as a story that happened to me, the story of a frustrating, nearly impossible, affection.

I was born in Dublin in 1948. My parents then lived in Pembroke Road in a flat [apartment] in a terraced house near the Grand Canal. My parents, who were, I think, instinctively city people, nevertheless decided to move to a fishing village to the north of Dublin when I was three years old. Howth offered sun, sea, wind, and great, green stretches of land. There was a lighthouse on the headland with a lighthouse keeper. There was a milkman who called with milk in a churn in the morning. The bread man came with his basket; "Vienna or batch or turnover?" he would ask.

Howth was a village then. Its harbor was lightly silted. It was a small place with small fishing, and grave granite buildings contemplated a calm sea. I can hardly bear to go back there now. The harbor has been given over to a mixture of deep-sea fishing and marina. The green stretches have been used for expensive suburban housing of the Dallas-out-of-Dynasty variety. Ranch-style neocolonial would be the best way to describe them.

But when I was growing up Howth was country and Dublin was town. It was something about the relationship of country to town that made me first fall in love with my surroundings in Howth and then transfer that love to the city. If you looked out of the front windows of our house on the top of Howth Hill, you had a broad and uninterrupted view of Dublin Bay and at night you could see a long curve of lights strung out like a necklace around the edge of the sea. I used to sit up in bed in the "sunporch" at home and send Morse-code signals to anyone who might be watching in Dun Laoghaire or Bray. The signals were never answered, but I felt that I was connected in some mysterious way with city life.

Of course we did go into Dublin. We had to. There were very few clothing stores in Howth. The shops were of the basic variety. If you wanted anything from shoes to school uniforms you went to town. We called Dublin a city then, but the process of moving towards it was "going into town." We went by tram and train and bus. I saw my first Sputnik sail through a starry sky from the open top of the Howth tram. The tram had a brass handle to steer it by, and the driver sometimes had to use a cloth on the rounded brass head of the handle to prevent his fingers from slipping. All those things, the tram, the train (antimacassars in first class) were part of the ritual that made going into town important. It was a long journey from the land of sea and gorse and heather to the city of the necklace, and you didn't slide through suburbia then. Your arrived, as it were, with a bang.

Dublin was not quite like the necklace place of my imagination when we got to it. It was shabby, poor, and vividly alive. You walked up Talbot Street from Amiens Street Station and you passed little shops selling everything from lucky bags to holy water fonts and the Child of Prague. I used to wonder why old people smelled funny in town. They smelled funny because so many of them lived in tenements without proper heating or hot water. You didn't wash very often if you had to heat water on a stove in a great cold building. I didn't know that then, but I could tell a poor person from a middle-class one and the difference frightened me.

But despite the widespread poverty and the terrible conditions in which people lived in working-class areas of the inner city, Dublin had a sense of community in the 1940s and 1950s. There used to be hundreds of people living over their shops in the Grafton Street and Henry Street areas of the city. Only a few dozen now remain. One Edward Kelly, who still lives in south King Street near St. Stephen's Green, remembers about three hundred people living in that street in the 1940s: "You were never lonely in that street. You could leave your door unlocked and no one would bother you. There was always someone around to keep an eye out." Middle-class people—the sort of people who now commute from the Dublin suburbs—also lived in Dublin then. My mother had a friend who lived in a fairly typical ground-floor flat in Merrion Square. The flat was a series of separate rooms arranged around a communal hallway. You unlocked doors with keys. One key for the kitchen here, a different key for the bathroom there, another key for the sitting room-bedroom at the back. It was inconvenient, but you could walk to work.

These days very few people live in Merrion Square. The "inconvenient" flats have been turned into offices. Middle-class people have become car owners who commute from leafy suburbs. The people who lived in the poorer areas of the inner city have been moved en masse to single-class suburbs. In the 1920s the population of the inner city was about a quarter of a million. By 1961 that had fallen to 160,000. By 1986—the year of the Dublin Crisis Conference—the number was estimated at 85,000, meaning that the population had been halved in twenty-five years.

One crucial event facilitated the move from living city to suburban sprawl. In 1964 two old tenements in Fenian Street collapsed, killing two little girls and causing a public outcry. In the eighteen months following the children's deaths, Dublin Corporation condemned two thousand buildings as "dangerous" and almost all of them were destroyed. No attempt was made to repair or restore them. Since most of the older buildings in the city center were built in terraces [rows] or squares, it was inevitable that the building next door to the "dangerous" building that had been demolished would become "dangerous" too. This process was sometimes encouraged by private landlords and property developers. If a building was not already "structurally" unsound, it could be made pretty dangerous by removing slates, lead flashing, and so on. The old tenements went, and in their place rose office blocks of varying degrees of hideousness interspersed by derelict sites whose owners were waiting for property prices to rise or for planning permission. Much of the central and north inner city has a blitzed appearance. Cranes and car parks proliferate. Whole terraces of fine, if shabby, Georgian buildings have been destroyed. Such destruction would have been unthinkable in any other European city—except in time of war. It could not have happened if large numbers of Irish people had not, in some way, wanted it to happen.

Irish people have, traditionally, thought of Dublin as being within the Pale, the area of immediate British influence. Though our Georgian squares and terraces were built by Irish builders and decorated and furnished by Irish craftsmen, the British taint was strong. Georgian Dublin was felt to be a foreign creation imposed on us by a colonizing power. When houses built for wealthy families were bought by private landlords and converted into tenements, the resulting slum conditions were seen as part of the British legacy. Poverty and slum conditions were added to the list of treasured wrongs that the British had caused us. Georgian Dublin reminded us of a state of powerlessness. Power lay in building and owning one's own property. A suburban house with garden front and back was the ideal of a rural people who had moved, with some reluctance, to the city. If you live in an apartment you have to share a building with other people. Irish people, who had memories of famine and emigration caused by eviction, did not want to share. They wanted to own every bit of the building they lived in, and they wanted to build something new to obliterate the memory of being owned.

The suburban ideal suited those middle-class people who could afford to buy their own houses and their own cars. It didn't suit working-class people who were moved out of the poorer areas of the inner city into single-class suburbs. The law allowed property developers to get rid of tenants in older buildings to clear sites for redevelopment. So thousands of tenants in the inner city were forced out of their homes with little or no compensation. After the Fenian Street episode, Dublin Corporation embarked on a huge and relentless slum clearance program that destroyed communities and broke up families. People were moved out of the city center and rehoused in the suburbs of Crumlin, Ballyfermot, and Ballymun and they weren't given much choice in the matter.

I doubt if anyone would have chosen to live in a drafty tenement with poor plumbing and inadequate heating. Some people protested that yes, they wanted better housing but they wanted it in the city, near people they'd always known. In sight of Mammy and Granny and Auntie. That choice wasn't on offer. The Irish solution to poverty in Dublin was to move it to the outskirts of the city where no one could see it. Unfortunately the towers of Ballymun, a high-rise development of system-built apartments, dominate the skyline like a series of sore thumbs. Everything that could go wrong did go wrong in Ballymun. The apartments—we call them flats—were either too hot or too cold. The lifts were vandalized and constantly out of order. Children fell to their deaths from the balconies, and adults threw themselves off them. Ironically, the towers of Ballymun were completed in 1969, just as architects and planners in other countries were beginning to realize that there might be something wrong with the whole concept of high-rise suburban development.

After Ballymun, which, it is now admitted, was an enormous and expensive failure, came the second phase, the "new-town-suburbs" of Tallaght, Lucan/Clondalkin, and Blanchardstown. This second phase is a mixture of public and private housing, and the houses conform more to a middle-class suburban ideal than the older single-class suburbs of Ballymun and Ballyfermot. House, garden front and back. Wide roads, wide enough, as someone said, so that two fire engines could pass each other traveling in opposite directions, which would be handy if you owned a fire engine or even a car. Tallaght is the biggest Dublin surburb. It is bigger than Limerick, Ireland's third-largest city. Yet Tallaght, which sprawls in rows of white houses across the foothills of the Dublin mountains, has no rail link. It has few local shops or pubs. For twenty years Tallaght waited for a town center. This year it got one. It's called The Square, a vast new shopping extravaganza with fountains, waterfalls, and glassy domes. The only trouble about The Square is getting there if you don't, as so many people in Tallaght don't, have a car. The wives of unemployed men share taxis to take them to The Square to do their weekly shopping. The view of the Dublin mountains from Tallaght is breathtaking. The houses are neat, the roads wide. Tallaght, most people who live there agree, would be all right if there were a proper rail link to and from the city center, or if you were rich and could afford a car and a freezer. Rich people do not live in Tallaght.

Even wealth doesn't help you to escape from Dublin's traffic problems. All along the coast from Howth to Bray (the sparkling necklace of my childhood imagination) runs the DART, a rapid rail transit system. People who live in those suburbs close to the DART can get in and out of town quickly and easily. If you don't live close to the DART, you wait for a bus that will get stuck in a traffic jam or you get into your own car and get stuck in a traffic jam. The solution to this problem is obvious. Dublin has become a suburban city that needs more rapid rail links. Not so, say the car owners. What Dublin needs is more motorways. Dublin now is turning into a motorway in search of a city center. Deirdre Kelly of the Living City Group, a Dublin pressure group that works for the preservation of the city, has remarked that "one can follow the proposed road plans by following the lines of dereliction" in innercity Dublin.

Compulsory purchase orders, which mark buildings for destruction, and rumors of motorway plans have turned large areas of the city into derelict sites and car parks. The trouble is that road engineers like roads more than they like cities. As far back as 1966 the British *Architect's Journal* pointed out that: "It is a sign of the old world . . . a view of planning held by Dublin Corporation that traffic is being treated as a separate issue."

Separate is a good word for Dublin. Dublin has become a separated city, and a city that is divided against itself cannot stand. Nowhere is this more obvious than in the different reactions of Dubliners—and I think of suburban Dublin people as Dubliners—to the various, if timid, improvements that have been made in the city. Some of the derelict sites have been filled in, usually with pastiche imitation-Georgian office buildings. At the corner of St. Stephen's Green rises an extraordinary and ambitious construction, a shopping mall called the Stephen's Green Centre. The Stephen's Green Centre is fantasy architecture tending towards the nostalgic and looks like a cross between Victorian Conservatory and Steamboat Gothic. Grafton Street has been pedestrianized and paved in red and black brick setts instead of the traditional granite slabs. Grafton Street looks quite pretty in a Christmas card way. Many Dubliners are pleased by these "improvements," which, they feel, are quaint without being shabby. In other words the fussy paving and even fussier street lights express a connection with a past that we simply did not have. They are "Olde English" rather than austere and authoritative British. They suggest village coziness rather than colonialism.

If people complain, as people who love the old city do complain, about the way in which pastiche is replacing the real thing, they are told that they are "begrudgers," not really Irish, but well-heeled, self-interested cranks who want to put a stop to development and progress. They are reminded that the Custom House has been restored and the Royal Hospital in Kilmainham too. They are told to look at the newly refurbished Government buildings and to admire the way in which the statues on top of the G.P.O. have been cleaned and repaired.

I admit that there have been improvements but they are, I think, more cosmetic than real. A building will be cleaned, restored, repaired, and so on if it is decided that it is an important building. We have, it seems, an awful lot of unimportant buildings in Dublin. The fact is that very little is being done to save the fabric of the city or to make those who care about that fabric feel that they have a right to care. It is as though we were content to polish the jewels of the crown while allowing the crown itself to disintegrate.

Recently, a group of European environmentalists came to Dublin to see the Iveagh Baths, a fine, Art Nouveau building near St. Patrick's Cathedral. There are rumors that the Iveagh Baths (which are in the care of Dublin Corporation) are in a dilapidated condition and in urgent need of restoration if they are to be saved. The European environmentalists did not get to see the Baths. Dublin Corporation refused them permission on the grounds that their motives were "political." Since the European environmentalists had made it quite clear that they wanted the Baths to be restored and preserved, I can only conclude that pleas for the preservation of this or that fine building are deemed to be "political" by Dublin Corporation.

Dubliners have lost more than fine Georgian buildings, they have lost the sense of safety and excitement that I spoke of earlier in this article. They have lost the feeling that they own their own city. When office development and motorway plans always come before the rights and needs of people who want to live, as well as work, in the city center, then the despair that comes from a sense of powerlessness sets in.

I feel that sense of despair every time I cross the Ha'penny Bridge. The Ha'penny Bridge is an elegantly arched pedestrian bridge spanning the Liffey upriver from O'Connell Bridge. From the Ha'penny Bridge you can see the Custom House (1791), Gandon's masterpiece, now overshadowed by the new Custom House Dock Development. You can also see great, ugly gaps in the charming rows of buildings that front on the quays. In any other European city these quayside houses would have been restored and turned into luxury flats or townhouses commanding high prices. In Dublin the quays are used for heavy traffic. It is impossible to stroll along the river without being deafened by the noise from articulated lorries and double-decker buses. The gaps in the rows of quayside houses are heartbreaking because they represent not just destruction but lost opportunity as well. It simply does not make sense, economically speaking, to destroy a unique tourist attraction.

But I know that the quays are being destroyed. I know I can do nothing to prevent them from being destroyed. Since I care about something that is being destroyed and since I am powerless to halt, or delay, the process of destruction, I try to avert my eyes every time I cross

Ha'penny Bridge. I want to stop caring. It's too painful to try to fight a battle that you know you are bound to lose.

My sixteen-year-old son was asked by his English teacher to write an essay about the view from O'Connell Bridge at six o'clock on a summer Sunday morning. This is what he wrote: "The sun rises above the docklands to the east, illuminating a new and ponderous intruder [the Customs House Dock Development]. A corporate fortress of gleaming, green glass burdening the pristine Custom House with its great mass. Along the quays, the morning light strikes buildings, leaving deep shadows on either side. These shadowed spaces, at first seeming natural, are places where houses once stood."

Perhaps one day I will be able to say that my son wrote an epitaph for Dublin before it died. The idea doesn't comfort me—much.

THERE IS
ALWAYS A RISK

ARMIN MAHLER
RICHARD RICKELMANN

Armin Mahler was born in Mühlacker, Germany. He has been an editor in the Economics Department of *Der Spiegel* since 1988. He is now one of the departmental directors.

Richard Rickelmann was born in Ibbenbüren, Germany. He has been an economic correspondent for *Der Spiegel* in Düsseldorf since 1975. Mr. Rickelmann currently lives in Solingen.

The following interview between Messrs. Mahler and Rickelmann and Jürgen Strubel, Chairman of the Board for the German chemical firm BASF, first appeared in *Der Spiegel*, in August 1991.

The head of BASF, Jürgen Strube, speaks about environmental damage and the responsibility of the chemical industry.

INTERVIEWER: Mr. Strube, for a year now you have been Chairman of the Board of Managing Directors at BASF and consequently one of the chemical industry's most powerful managers in the world. Do you find this a burdensome responsibility?

STRUBE: I share the responsibility with my colleagues on the Board. Furthermore, we work together with our BASF regional directors, which gives us a broad base for the successful management of such a large operation.

INTERVIEWER: We are referring more to your responsibility as a representative of an industrial branch that contributes to the destruction of the earth.

STRUBE: That is a misrepresentation that I must reject. The chemical industry contributes significantly to the industrial nations' enjoyment of a prosperity never before experienced. The industry also aids developing countries by seeking to solve their critical problems. The chemical industry offers indisputable support with regard to questions of nutrition, hygiene, and medicine.

INTERVIEWER: But the industry's success stories are peppered with scandals. Rivers, lakes, and seas are contaminated. Forests are dying. The climate threatens to collapse. Doesn't this disturb you?

STRUBE: Such a sweeping accusation unjustifiably holds the entire chemical industry accountable. The chemical sector is part of our industrialized world. Some criticism is justified. However, one should not point a finger solely at the chemical industry.

INTERVIEWER: Must we also exclude then the pesticides in drinking water, the dioxin and heavy metals in food, the increase in environmentally caused illnesses such as allergies and cancer, and the growing mountains of waste? Don't these problems give you cause for concern?

Jürgen Strube is the first non-chemist to head Germany's largest chemical establishment. The 52-year-old lawyer started with BASF in 1969, after which he spent considerable time out of the country, mostly in Brazil. In 1985 he was elected to the Board of Directors and was relocated to the United States. In 1990 he assumed the position of Chairman of the Board. Strube has a much more agreeable demeanor than his predecessor, Hans Albers; however, when it comes down to it he is equally demanding.

The BASF Group, with a turnover of $82 billion and 135,000 employees, is one of the world's largest companies in the chemical industry, second only to DuPont. Nevertheless, the comfortable years for BASF and its competitors, Bayer and Hoechst, seem to be over. Turnover and profits faltered during the first half of 1991. Strube hopes to move the firm toward specialization in its most lucrative areas.

STRUBE: Every manifestation of civilization that proves damaging gives cause for concern. That does not even need to be discussed. However, in terms of the points you have raised we first have to determine the causes and categorize them. From there we can determine all the possible approaches that could be taken to remedy the situation.

INTERVIEWER: For example, don't you find the increase in superfluous synthetic packaging materials to be an obvious factor behind the growing piles of nonbiodegradable waste?

STRUBE: No, the proportion of man-made materials in so-called household waste comprises only six to seven percent. Every discussion of synthetic packaging materials should begin with this number. Incidentally, in Germany we have found an altogether sensible approach to this problem by trying to avoid, minimize, and eventually make use of waste products. This opens up a number of opportunities for restructuring that today are only in the beginning stages.

INTERVIEWER: What are you specifically referring to?

STRUBE: Recycling, for example. The incineration of garbage to generate energy also makes sense. In this way we can reduce direct petroleum consumption. Synthetic materials are, after all, little more than borrowed energy. We therefore have the chance to use oil derivatives two, three, or even four times.

INTERVIEWER: You talk as if recycling of man-made materials is common everywhere. As a rule, packaging lands on a dump heap. It does not decompose, and in a thousand years it will still be lying in the earth.

STRUBE: Synthetic products are far too valuable to land on a dump. And by the way, your statement is incorrect. Recycling is also done with synthetic substances.

INTERVIEWER: To a small extent.

STRUBE: But increasingly. The synthetic waste material produced during the manufacturing process is being turned into something useful. Greater cooperation is being shown by automobile and styrofoam manufacturers in regard to return and recycling procedures. However, synthetic materials are not recycled at the level of steel or iron, for example. To some degree this is because recycling of synthetic materials is much costlier. We will have to find new ways of achieving our goal.

INTERVIEWER: This all sounds, though, as if the chemical industry and its products do no harm whatever to the environment. To quote from a report of the German government on what flows into the North Sea every year: 11,000 tons of lead, 28,000 tons of zinc, 335 tons of cadmium, 75 tons of mercury, 150,000 tons of oil, 100,000 tons of phosphate, and so on.

STRUBE: But do those figures reflect the total damage done to the North Sea—from every tributary and from the atmosphere too?

INTERVIEWER: Yes, that's correct.

STRUBE: Then you should not attribute total damage solely to the role played by the chemical industry. For example, the major portion of lead pollution originates from automobile exhaust that escapes out over the North Sea. Since the time those figures were originally compiled—that was between 1983 and 1986—we have accomplished quite a lot.

INTERVIEWER: For example?

STRUBE: We can present very satisfying statistics to show how the chemical industry and especially BASF have drastically reduced the level of pollution in the Rhine River. The remaining content of chromium and copper in BASF's sewage plant effluent remains at the acceptable level for drinking water. Mercury and cadmium levels are actually below the required levels. In the past ten years we have reduced air pollution by 60%. That is a very significant improvement.

INTERVIEWER: The chemical industry likes to boast of its successes in regard to environmental protection. But these successes are brought about mostly by expectations and conditions set by officials.

STRUBE: As long ago as the 1950s BASF began developing plans for a large purification plant. It has been operating since 1974. We did this willingly with no pressure from government authorities. Therefore it cannot be said that only critics of the chemical industry are responsible for the success of environmental protection efforts.

INTERVIEWER: Has it ever occurred to you that the price we have to pay for the benefits of the chemical industry could be too high?

STRUBE: The relationship between cost, benefit, and risk is always up for scrutiny. There are always various views as to what situation is acceptable. We are currently experiencing a shift in values to which we must get accustomed. Some of what seemed acceptable in the past is no longer so today.

INTERVIEWER: Can you name an example from your various companies?

STRUBE: Of course this change in values also occurs within our establishment. You can see that by the fact that we have expanded the notion of environmental protection in our firm's central management into a goal that is equally valued throughout the entire establishment.

INTERVIEWER: What does that mean in practice?

STRUBE: It means that for ecological reasons an ecologically necessary action cannot fall by the wayside. As a result, a consensus between science, technology, and politics must be reached on the ecological necessity itself.

INTERVIEWER: That sounds good. However, mistrust of the chemical industry runs very deep. Accidents and breakdowns were hushed up and denied for so long even when the proof was painfully obvious.

STRUBE: I cannot speak for other companies, only for BASF. And certainly, your reproach in our case is unwarranted.

INTERVIEWER: Perhaps the industry could have avoided a lot of damage if, for example, news on dioxin had been made available at the right time.

STRUBE: We reported our findings. I would especially like to remind you that extraordinary progress has been made in the technological development of measuring techniques. There are methods for detecting materials that were not available just a few years ago. Yet, having proof of material traces does not imply immediate danger. The investigation into the possible side effects of new products has become much more intensive.

INTERVIEWER: Does such reasoning or investigation actually render dangerous substances harmless?

STRUBE: Undesired side effects cannot be completely ruled out. There always remains a certain risk, even if small.

INTERVIEWER: Have you ever removed a product from the market because it was too dangerous?

STRUBE: Yes, not just once. BASF has taken well over 100 products out of circulation for environmental or work-security related reasons.

INTERVIEWER: However, you continue to manufacture many products about which scientists have expressed caution, for example organic chlorine combinations. Is that really necessary?

STRUBE: The individual members of this class of substances have very disparate qualities. When unwanted effects on health and the environment have become apparent we have discontinued production. For example, trichlorphenol and dichlorphenol. Most of the chlorine products manufactured here at the Ludwigshafen site are processed internally. There are certainly some that can be replaced. And there are some for which there is no replacement.

INTERVIEWER: For example, fluorocarbons, which are responsible for the hole in the ozone layer.

STRUBE: Fluorocarbons have never been manufactured by BASF.

INTERVIEWER: But they are still being produced in Germany.

STRUBE: No other country on earth has, like Germany, laid down the law by renouncing the production and use of fluorocarbons until 1995. German industry has already replaced them for the most part. And since the middle of 1990 the foam material Styrodur at BASF has been manufactured with a new propellant. With that a 95% reduction in the ozone-damaging potential can be achieved. I see this as a step in the right direction. The manufacture of these replacement products, of course, calls for significant research.

INTERVIEWER: The discussion on polyvinyl chloride (PVC) is just beginning. When will BASF be taking this product off the market?

STRUBE: BASF is seen internationally as a marginal PVC manufacturer. As such, we can certainly discontinue production of this material more readily than others. Yet PVC has a quality profile that makes it thoroughly appealing for various areas of application. Also here one has to weigh the benefits against possible damages.

INTERVIEWER: That, of course, means it could be easy for you to benefit from its use and the general public to feel the impact of the damage.

STRUBE: How do you come to the conclusion that predominant use is by those companies supplying PVC?

INTERVIEWER: You make the gains and the general public bears the burden of waste management.

STRUBE: Waste management was considered a community responsibility even in ancient Roman times. We are now possibly facing a turning point at which this traditional sharing of responsibility is being revised.

INTERVIEWER: What is your opinion on a waste tax?

STRUBE: I could only say if I knew the development, goal orientation, and the consignee of such a tax. Above all, at present a waste tax is being discussed as a financial opportunity to combat old debts in the new German states. These burdens belong to us all and may not be ascribed only to a certain sector of the supplying industry.

INTERVIEWER: You are not against such a tax in general?

STRUBE: Taxes such as these should have a directional function. Whether this directional focus is successful is initially an open question. These days the government is inclined to use these taxes as a source of revenue. And every new source of revenue is temptation for new projects.

INTERVIEWER: If the costs of waste management are not calculated into the price paid by the consumer and thus taken care of, then future generations will have to raise the money. Shouldn't the generation that causes the damage pay?

STRUBE: First of all, products fulfill market demand and do not themselves cause damage. Otherwise no one would buy them. When these market demands are satisfied then...

INTERVIEWER: ...the damages appear.

STRUBE: That can happen in particular cases; however, it is not the rule. When waste remains, who is responsible for the costs? Is it the final consumer, or is it the supplier? Is the manufacturer who processes the raw materials or the original supplier of these materials responsible?

INTERVIEWER: That was a question. How do you answer it?

STRUBE: The answer should primarily be provided by legislators.

INTERVIEWER: You could help them out.

STRUBE: The German economy is taking a dual approach to this. I am very much of the opinion that we should generate energy from household waste by using waste power stations. In that way we would no longer have a shortage in disposal sites and at the same time could produce energy.

INTERVIEWER: The consumer's behavior might change if he were better informed about the harmful substances in products and the possibilities available for waste management. Why does your enterprise resist labeling its products more thoroughly?

STRUBE: I support that in cases where it makes sense, for example with synthetic materials. However, the components of many products are a combination of substances. Would you want to label a tie showing what dyes were used?

INTERVIEWER: Certainly information can be attached stating whether materials can be recycled.

STRUBE: That information by itself serves little purpose, because almost all materials can be recycled. I also believe that one should take advantage of the opportunity with synthetic materials to make repeated use of oil derivatives. This makes sense ecologically and economically.

INTERVIEWER: And the prices of products not included in this category should then be raised?

STRUBE: The market will determine that.

INTERVIEWER: The chemical industry has all of these problems under control, and the market will settle things by itself—according to your reasoning, any criticism of your enterprise would be labeled hysteria?

STRUBE: Of course, it's not that simple. A significant reason for criticism is based on the fact that the benefit of using many chemicals is not easily perceivable. Goods are simply produced, and in the end the relation between their beneficial use and any original chemical components can no longer be determined.

INTERVIEWER: As the Chairman of the Board of Directors you are obligated to the shareholders. You must show successful results.

STRUBE: At the most recent meeting I reasserted that we are obligated as much to the shareholders as to all our employees and the general public.

INTERVIEWER: You do not see any conflict of interest in that?

STRUBE: The long-term goals of the company should by all means be harmonized with the wishes and demands of society. It always goes back to the fundamental question: How can we feed a growing population—at the end of the century the world population will have grown by almost one billion—how can we maintain their good health, how can we offer all of humanity a life worth living? The chemical industry plays a very important role in all of these matters. With its help we can intensify the use of many scarce resources in the world, in a manner that would not be possible without the chemical industry's help.

INTERVIEWER: And your shareholders are satisfied with that?

STRUBE: Some shareholders are of course more interested in short-term maturity and high profits. Again, the public makes demands on us that limit our flexibility in balancing the demands of the employees and the shareholders. One of my tasks is to find a reasonable solution to this problem.

INTERVIEWER: Mr. Strube, we thank you for this interview.

Translated by Heidi Whitesell

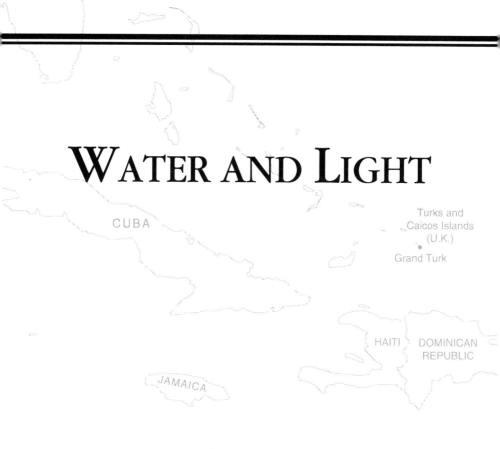

WATER AND LIGHT

CUBA

Turks and
Caicos Islands
(U.K.)
Grand Turk

HAITI   DOMINICAN
REPUBLIC

JAMAICA

Caribbean Sea

STEPHEN HARRIGAN

VENEZUELA

COLOMBIA

Stephen Harrigan was born in Oklahoma City, Oklahoma. He is is the author of two novels, *Aransas* and *Jacob's Well,* and a collection of essays, *A Natural State.* His articles and essays have been featured in a number of publications, including *Esquire, Life,* and the *New York Times Magazine.* Mr. Harrigan is a contributing editor for *Texas Monthly.* He has been awarded a grant from the National Endowment for the Arts as well as a Dobie-Paisano Fellowship. His screenplay, *Ishi,* is currently in production.

The following selection is an excerpt from his forthcoming book, *Water and Light,* to be published by Houghton Mifflin in May 1992.

Mr. Harrigan lives in Austin, Texas, with his wife, Sue Ellen, and three daughters, Marjorie, Dorothy, and Charlotte.

I walked down Front Street, along the edge of the sea. The night was clear and still, the ocean a heaving shadow interrupted by streaks of phosphorescence and the running lights of a handful of boats. It was Saturday night, but downtown Cockburn Town was almost deserted. A light westerly wind coasted in off the water, driving six-inch waves that slapped softly against the pilings. I could smell sea wrack, garbage, decay from the salinas, and deep-fat frying from the Poop Deck restaurant. In the center of the street a wild donkey brayed, a sound like a creaking hinge swung violently back and forth.

From the open doors of St. Mary the Virgin Anglican Episcopal Church, whose white lime facade gleamed in the darkness, I could hear the sounds of choir practice, a host of Black voices singing the British Empire's sonorous hymns of faith. Listening to the hymns, to the braying of the donkey, I walked out onto a rickety pier and stood gazing down at the dark water. Even after weeks of constant diving, the world beneath its surface seemed utterly secret, my memories of it regularly threatening to vanish. The reef itself, not just the water that covered it, was a fluid presence in my mind. When I was on the surface, landmarks of the reef presented themselves to my imagination like a taunting memory of childhood, like some moody, exotic place glimpsed through sleepy eyes at the age of three or four—a place that you will never see again or even clearly remember, but that will call to you mysteriously from some deep chamber of your mind.

It always surprised me a little to find these landmarks still there when I slipped over the side of the boat. To see them again was like going to sleep and reentering the landscape of a dream from the night before. Out of the water, out of that dream, I was habitually restless. Tonight, as always, I feared I was missing something. I was anxious about the things that were going on without my knowledge beneath that dark water.

The island itself I had barely noticed; Grand Turk, one of the tiny islands comprising the British Commonwealth colony of Turks and Caicos, was just a platform for jumping into the sea. Now, though, as I walked through Cockburn Town, listening to the Anglican choir sing "My Father's God to Thee," the island finally began to claim my attention. I climbed on board my scooter and rode around aimlessly in the night.

I ended up on the opposite side of the island, standing on the summit of the limestone ridge looking out at the barrier reef to windward. I could see the faint line of surf beyond the lagoon, and the scant moonlight softened the raw gray rock on which I stood.

I looked down into the water, watching the waves collide against the rock, hitting its hollow pockets with a sharp clap and sending up a plume of spray. It was late, but the desire to be below the surface was irresistible. I jumped on the scooter and rode back to my hotel, gathered my mask, snorkel, fins, and an underwater light, and walked down to the beach.

Hummocks of dried turtle grass, uprooted from the lagoon and washed ashore by the waves, stretched all along the beach. Walking through the grass in my neoprene booties, I could feel shells and crustacean pieces crunching beneath my feet. The water was warm enough—no need for a wet suit if I kept moving—but the lagoon was shallow, and I had to walk twenty or thirty yards in knee-deep water until the terrain sloped enough for me to submerge. I slipped my face beneath the water and looked around before turning on my light.

I was in a landscape of soft steely light, the moonlight washing through the waves and illuminating the sand flats and distant coral boulders with sumptuous hues of gray. The wind whistled through my snorkel. I felt my body rocking gently, buoyant in the waves. The world was colorless but welcoming, an enfolding darkness full of unexpected texture and richness.

After a moment I turned on the light. The beam fell on a waving bed of turtle grass, from which thick, fan-shaped growths of algae protruded. Here in the grass beds and sand flats there was little color, even with the light beam to coax it out. The grass and algae had merely a dark greenish tint, the sand was white, the occasional sea cucumbers as brown and russety as baked potatoes.

Swimming out into deeper water, I took a breath and dived to the bottom, cruising above the ripples in the sand or following the snail tracks to see where they might lead. Tiny, frantic fish skirted around me, and when they crossed the beam of light their shadows were projected onto the sand many times their size, so that I felt surrounded by some undefinable fluttering movement, like the anxious beating of bat wings.

I had often dived at night, though always with scuba gear and never alone. But snorkeling now through the dark sand flats made me feel exposed and edgy, and whenever I came up for air I was struck with how much more vulnerable I felt at the surface than below. With a scuba tank on my back I always had a sense of being armored and full of options. I could hide behind a rock, wedge myself into a crevice until whatever had scared me lost interest and swam away.

I was far from terror tonight, but I couldn't shake a vague apprehension. I had fallen into a suggestible mood, and I thought I could feel things cruising about in the water with me, just out of the range of my available senses. It was as if the ocean itself were an exquisitely sensitive trap and every move I made set off a vibration that alerted the unseen beast residing at its center. There was no danger, just the uncomfortable closeness of the night, pressing in.

Many of the daytime herbivores were asleep now, or as close to sleep as fish get: holed up in a crevice, canted motionless to one side, their minds locked in some monotonous waking dream. But the carnivorous night shift was out—the cardinalfish and squirrelfish with their big, liquid, night-perfect eyes; the spotted morays rippling through the coral underbrush; the lobsters prowling along the bottom with ghostly, delicate movements of their many limbs. I saw a deep linear gouge in the sand—like the tread of an off-road tire—and followed it for a while, hoping to find the sizable sting ray that had made it. But I lost the trail when my attention was diverted by a porcupinefish. These boxy fish, covered with spines, have the sort of mild, expressive features you see on the faces of the valiant trucks and tugboats in children's picture books.

Porcupinefish, along with puffers or blowfish, which resemble them, are inflatable. They can instantly gulp enough water to expand like a balloon, driving their spines into the mouth of an attacker.

Had I felt like being bothersome, I would have provoked this one into inflating itself, but I was careful about my manners tonight, nervous about the dark sea brooding in judgment over my every move. And I liked watching the porcupinefish swim about in its unexcited state, its fins whirring furiously to keep its body upright. It moved seemingly without volition, in teetering, tilting motions, as if powered by a gyroscope.

As I drew closer to a scattered series of coral heads, the smooth sand bottom gave way to rubbly terrain, and I saw an octopus moving like a stream of mercury across the rocks. The octopus was small—a foot and a half across, probably, from arm tip to arm tip—but it was such a restless, slithering mass that size seemed irrelevant. Like a gas, it could be measured only by estimating its volume.

I crept up behind it, watching it change colors as it slid over the rocks—in an instant it turned from white, to lavender, to a warty institutional green. Its head was floppy and bulbous, like some grotesque tumor, and its eight radiating arms were joined for half their length by a rippling membrane of flesh. The octopus had not seen me and was not in a hurry. It proceeded with elegant fluidity, one arm after another flung forward in a movement that reminded me of the slow-motion cracking of a bullwhip. Unlike their squid cousins, octopuses are not particularly adept swimmers; they're crawlers. They move by probing with their arms and gaining purchase on the substrate with their thousands of powerful suction disks.

They are capable, however, of sharp bursts of velocity. When I reached down and touched this one it instantly turned brick red, let out a cloud of ink, emitted a blast of water from its funnel, and shot upward, its eight arms trailing like streamers from its wobbling head. It landed several yards away and poured itself into a hole no more than a few inches in diameter. One arm then flashed out of the hole, twirled around a nearby beer can, and drew it in front of the opening to block my approach. I pulled on the beer can to test the creature's grip; it might have been cemented into place.

The beer can did not totally cover the entrance to the lair, and when I shone my light through the tiny opening I could see, glaring out at me from the darkness, one of the most awesome sights in all nature: the eye of an octopus.

An octopus is an invertebrate. It is a mollusk, like a garden slug or an oyster. But unlike most mollusks, which see only through blotches of light-sensitive pigment, an octopus has a remarkably complex eye, complete with iris, retina, pupil, lens, cornea. The octopus eye, we assume, sees more or less what the human eye would see, and like the human eye it not only receives but emits. It takes in light, forms images, and sends out expressions of mood and thought. When you look eye to eye with an octopus, something clicks. You feel it staring at you, taking your measure, *thinking* about you. There is a disturbing, almost unspeakable recognition. You realize that the octopus's eye, like yours, is the window of its soul.

Of its soul? Perhaps this eye, with its weird familiarity, its brooding awareness, merely deceives us into believing that the octopus has a reverberant consciousness to go with it. But it is no illusion, I think, that the octopus has a temperament, that it is governed by fitful storms of emotion so powerful and sweeping that they seem to emanate from some source larger than the compressed knot of ganglia that serves as the creature's brain. An octopus is easy to rile, easy to scare. It announces its state of mind by instantaneous changes of color, the muscle-activated pigment cells in its skin compressing and expanding like the pixels on an electronic scoreboard.

I remembered an octopus I had encountered several years earlier, when I was diving off a boat in the Gulf of Mexico. I had been sitting on deck, waiting to go down again, when a member of our group surfaced cradling an octopus in his arms like a baby. He got into the boat, filled a deep ice chest with seawater, put the octopus inside, and jumped overboard to resume his dive. I was the only person on deck. The diver had said nothing about his plans for the octopus, and since I was fairly sure they were not in the animal's best interests I thought about letting it back into the water. I was still considering when I saw a tentacle drape itself over the edge of the ice chest. Very slowly and stealthily the rest of the octopus followed. Balanced on the styrofoam rim, it paused and moved its eyes. I saw it looking at me, not a blind stare but a knowing assessment of risk. The octopus, I was sure, was taking stock of its situation. Finally it poured itself onto the deck and, without hesitation but also without evident hurry, slithered to the transom of the boat and calmly disappeared.

This octopus, the one I had cornered now in its lair, regarded me with the same air of calculation. It seemed to be thinking to itself: *What will happen to me now?* But it had calmed down, subsiding back to a mottled gray hue, more or less secure in its home base. Octopuses are extremely attached to their dwellings. "One of the main preoccupations of the octopus," writes Jacques Cousteau, "is to maintain a point of contact with its rock or its hole. From this contact, it derives strength and confidence."

Octopus holes are clean and smooth inside, swept clear of debris by periodic blasts of water from the octopus's funnel. Outside they are junkyards, littered with old crab parts, bits of coral, or other objects the octopus has collected or cast off. Sometimes the octopus walls off the opening, building a rampart of shell or stone. Its need for a close, smooth, secret place into which it can pour its liquid body is apparently intense. Octopuses routinely harbor themselves in the amphorae and pots of ancient shipwrecks. They have been known to escape the rect-angular glass panes of aquarium tanks to slip into teapots. This need to secure themselves within burrows strikes me as a primordial insecurity, a need to return to the protective shell that once covered their ancestors and that evolution took away before the creatures inside—so shapeless, so appallingly naked—were ready to be exposed.

But they are far from defenseless. Caught in the open, they can instantaneously change color—even change texture—to blend into the background. When startled they eject a cloud of ink to mask their escape, like a magician disappearing behind a puff of stage smoke. As predators they are armed with excellent eyesight, their bodies are unbelievably supple and muscular, their arms and sucker disks are exquisitely sensitive to touch and chemical

129

sensation. They can snatch a crab with a single arm from the cover of their hole, or they can leap up and descend upon it with their mantle flared like a malevolent parachute. Their mouth is a hard bony beak, like a parrot's, and a small octopus can spurt poison from its salivary glands potent enough to kill a rabbit. When they eat a crab or a lobster they send their probing, flexible arms deep into its crevices, conveying the meat out along the sucker disks and leaving behind an almost unbroken, hollow shell.

Octopuses are solitary. They never congregate and generally can't seem to stand the sight of one another. But they mate with languorous absorption, clinging to each other for hours. The male has a specialized arm called a hectocotylus with a groove in the center, which he inserts into the body cavity of the female. The mating itself has a kind of loading-bay quality to it—the male delivering sperm packets at regular intervals down the groove, the female receiving them and warehousing them in her oviduct.

Afterwards they part company. He slithers off to business as usual. She returns to her lair to lay her eggs, brood them, and die. There are many thousands of eggs encased in long white tubes, which the mother octopus hangs from the ceiling of the hole like icicles. While her young are developing she does not eat. Her will is streamlined to a maternal obsession so total that it can end only in death. She cleans the egg cases with her arms and with blasts of air from her funnel. Though she weakens daily, she rouses herself to chase off potential predators. When the young hatch, there may be a quarter million of them, a cloud of pinhead-sized baby octopuses drifting out of the hole where their mother lies depleted and dying.

Octopuses sometimes eat their own arms and grow them back. They can also regenerate their eyes. Their own ink is toxic to them, but they have been observed to walk through a beachside campfire with no apparent discomfort. Octopuses are susceptible to hypnosis and if stared at long enough turn as limp as mops. The surest way to kill one is to bite down hard between its eyes.

Many species of octopus, some of them still probably unknown, inhabit the world's oceans. Far below in the abyss, as deep as three miles, live blind octopuses with translucent, gossamer tissues. The blue-ringed octopus, found in the waters of Australia, has a venomous bite that has proved fatal to humans. Reports of giant octopuses tend toward the folkloric, but such creatures apparently do exist. A partial specimen that washed ashore at St. Augustine, Florida, reportedly had an arm length of 75 to 90 feet.

There is no particular reason to fear octopuses, but occasional "attacks" have occurred in which an octopus impulsively whipped out an arm or two and pinioned a passing bather. Once an Australian parson, leading a group of boys in a walk along the Victoria seashore, had the peculiar experience of being set upon by an octopus that crawled right out of the water to grab him around the legs and waist. (He beat it off with a fishing rod.) Certainly a surprise encounter of this sort is an unsavory experience. "My mouth was smothered by some flabby moving horror," recounts one traumatized octopus wrestler. "The suckers felt like hot rings pulling at my skin. It was only two seconds, I suppose...but it seemed like a century of nausea." But anyone who has ever come across an octopus in open water, watched it spurt its ink and slink deep into its hole, its eyes full of fear and its chromatic skin flashing in alarm, knows that a deliberate attack is a wildly improbable event.

I was not frightened of octopuses, but more than any other creature on the reef they haunted my imagination. And tonight, as I shone my light into the hole and stared at that eye with its eerie black rectangular pupil, I was startled by a feeling as intense as an electric shock. The octopus did not just have a brain, it had a mind. And that mind, unthinkably alien, was trained on me. A thought was passing between us. The eye looking out at me was filled with fear and disdain, and its message was as clear as if it had been spoken: Go away.

SOUNDING THE ECOLOGICAL ALARM

SVETLANA VISHNEVSKAYA

Svetlana Vishnevskaya was born near Kaluga, Russia, and was raised in the Ukraine. She received a bachelor of science degree in geology from the University of Moscow. Ms. Vishnevskaya lived for six years in Washington, D.C., where her late husband, Sergei Vishnevskii, worked as a journalist for *Pravda*.

Ms. Vishnevskaya is an environmental journalist for *Komsomolskaya Pravda*, a newspaper for teenagers notable for its speaking out in support of Mikhail Gorbachev during the coup attempt of August 1991. Her work has been featured in several newspapers and periodicals, and she will soon publish a book about the national parks of the world.

Ms. Vishnevskaya lives in Moscow. She has two children, Nikolai and Ivan.

As an environmental journalist I have had the pleasure of discovering that thousands of newspaper readers in the USSR are finding ways to prevent an apocalypse and to preserve the environment.

Five years ago, at the beginning of the environmental movement here, I was drawn on a trip by a letter I received from a young reader, Vitalii Loginov, who lives in the village of Dubky, near Yaroslavl. He wrote: "There is a new Yaroslavl oil refinery near Dubky that, along with the nearby technical carbon plant, is poisoning all the inhabitants of this area."

I decided to see for myself. One spring day I stepped off the train from Moscow and caught a bus in Yaroslavl.

The bus drove for a while beside a concrete wall that I found somehow disquieting. But this grim wall was a picket fence compared with the two structures within its embrace. Through the window of the bus I saw a circus of pipes, chimneys, and ducts. Together, the two plants described by Vitalii Loginov looked like a huge musical monster that no one remembers how to play. Power issued from its chinks and apertures—sometimes as white noiseless smoke, sometimes as whistling steam, driving hard along the whole length of the metal labyrinth. It gathered into columns of smoke that filled the whole sky, blocking out the sun.

You begin to understand a lot of things about ecology when you pass the oil refinery. You understand not with your mind, but with your skin, and you begin almost to shrivel because of your biological inferiority to this steaming armored plant. Vitalii had written: "Regularly, especially in the summer, these two plants release a very unpleasant smelling gas. All of this happens at night."

Walking around the village, past two- and three-story buildings, I asked some of the citizens of Dubky their opinions about the pollution. One middle-aged woman straightened the scarf on her head and looked at me with curiosity: "What can I do? I am just a mortal. The only thing to do is to close the window and continue to live." I stopped an old woman who was hurrying somewhere in loose rubber boots. "What is it like to live here? They fill the area with gas and my husband becomes covered with red spots. He tells me that they are testing us to see if we will survive." A young woman with a bicycle fell to thinking for a moment: "Certainly, it's very unpleasant, but I'm sure that someone will do something to put an end to all these explosions and accidents. But what can I do by myself? I can't imagine what I can do about it." A man with a large bag did not even want to listen to the question: "I know nothing. I saw nothing. It's not my problem," he said and walked away, proud that he did not deviate from the pre-*glasnost* Soviet line.

Not long before, four tons of soot had fallen on the four thousand inhabitants of Dubky, two pounds per person, during the only accident that ever occurred at the plants. "And now the linen that was hanging to dry on the clothesline can only be used to wipe the back stairs," housewives told me. The local poet screwed up his eyes and recited: "Dogs are losing their color; trees, their characteristics; and snow, its shadows."

I found the home of the young writer of the letter and met his family. Vitalii's concern for the environment, I soon learned, came from his mother and father. He wanted to become a chemist and protect the environment.

That meeting sank deep in my mind. As long as we have such people there is hope that ecological accidents will not become commonplace occurrences. It is wonderful to believe that good will conquer because a 14-year-old boy in Dubky is lying awake at night and decrying our ecological folly. The same thing is occurring all over the country. Sadly, on this score our national ministries and departments have been virtual foreigners in their native country.

But these are complicated matters. My mailbox is swollen with letters from concerned readers. Some of them are monotonous, some are illegible, some are ten pages long, some turn me into a dark pessimist. But all support the hope that even if the situation does not improve immediately, nature will defend itself, and we have a future.

Articles and letters cannot change the environment overnight, but their role is significant. Long live letters! "I am 31 years old," writes Sergei Kliucharov. "I am Karelian, living in the Karelian Peninsula. My letter will not discuss my salary (which is so small, you would not believe me if I told you, and that would make you doubt everything else I have to say). I am not writing about the products that are not in the stores. And not about the prices of products, when I must work almost three days to buy two pounds of sausage. That is only information for reflection. My letter is about the main resource of my Karelia—the forest. The forest is gone! Do you understand? It is missing. It was cut down and destroyed. "

Expressions of concern over the loss of forests are reaching our editorial office from all over the country. "The Carpathian forests," writes engineer Viktor Oksinenko, "were always known for their fine air quality, so health centers, public facilities, and youth camps were built there. I went to see the beauty of the Carpathian forests, glorified in so many songs, but all my hopes were dashed in a single moment. The forest had been cut down. Heaps of untidy boughs were left behind. People in a nearby village told me that until recently state supervision of the Carpathian forests had prevented logging. It had been illegal even for villagers to cut down a tree for New Year's. But the large trees of the forest had been transferred to the local authority of *kolkhozes**. This was someone's understanding of democratization. Thousands of hectares were obliterated as kolkhozes cleared them to gain 420 rubles for each meter of wood. They did not replant the stripped forest, nor did they use any of their earnings to maintain the forest. Felled trees, their boughs still attached, were pushed out of the forest with bulldozers, destroying everything in their path. Will this go unpunished?"

Most of the anxious letters about the disappearing forests come from the Russian republic, which is heavily wooded. The total area of felled forests increased sevenfold over the last decade, according to our statistics.

Forests are not the only victims. Rivers and lakes, the jewels of nature, were the first to be sacrificed in the ecological tragedy.

Fifth-grade pupils from a Ukrainian village write: "There is now a lot of awareness about the ecological situation. That's why we are writing about the fate of our nearby river (if it is still possible to call it that). It changed into a sewage canal for neighboring businesses in front of our eyes. And our river runs into the Dnepr, poisoning all its flora and fauna. The inhabitants of our village use this water on their kitchen window gardens. Sometimes, the river catches fire when a match or cigarette butt is tossed into it. We feel that we are witnessing the final stage of an ecological disaster. The death of the river is a terrible symptom."

To comprehend the scale of the pollution affecting small rivers, it is enough to note that, according to statistics, approximately one third have such high levels of pollution that they meet or exceed the official maximum permissible concentration ten times over.

---

kolkhoz—Russian for "collective farm."

The Aral Sea is drying up. Aleksander Fedosenko writes from Kazakhstan: "As you know, the Aral Sea is fed by two rivers, the Syr Daria and the Amu Daria. The largest tributary of the Syr Daria, the Arys River, flows through our town. According to the newspapers, a decision was made to let as much water into the sea as possible and to divert as little as possible for economic needs. But some land was earmarked for construction of summer houses not far from the city, and the decision was made to provide them with water from the Arys River, which is already shallow. They are now building the pumping station to pump water for country houses. Is it possible that the river and the sea will be ruined for this small convenience?"

But from our letters we see that concern about saving lakes, rivers, and forests, while extremely strong, is less than our readers' worry about saving animals.

"This is Yurii Sidorov from Odessa writing to you." We are reading children's letters written on paper from a school copybook. "Someone injured a dolphin. It threw itself onto the bank, but people did not want to help it. There are very angry, stale, and indifferent people living in Odessa...I am very upset about the dolphin. You see, people had to help him, but they did not want to."

A letter comes from the Ussuriiskii area. It may especially interest Western readers. "It is paradise here, fresh air, taiga*, hills," writes Valentin Artiushenko. "I recently learned that during a year-long hunting exchange foreign hunters are to be allowed to kill old (?) bears, deer, and other animals. It is interesting: How will foreign hunters determine the age of the animal from a distance? Perhaps all of these animals are marked? But I want you to understand me. I am not against their coming here, to hunt, to vacation. It is a good thing and it would even be inter-

---

*taiga—coniferous evergreen forests of subarctic lands.

139

esting to find out who they are, these Westerners. But all the same I would be glad if the majority of them preferred films and photographs about hunting to hunting animals."

As I quote this letter, I question whether it is a good idea to publish letters without special insights, with private issues, generalizations, and intellectual flights. But this letter was candid, like one written to a friend. If my essay helps Western readers to understand the true faces of my compatriots even a little, my task will be accomplished.

The environmental movement in our country is still being formed. It is only the beginning. It is changing in this age of public participation, which has a place for everyone.

"I hope," writes young engineer M. Ponomarev of Piatigorsk, "that our people will have access to comprehesive environmental information. I think that if alternative social and economic development plans are published, and if plans are prepared in an open process that involves the public, we will make fewer environmental mistakes. Complicated scientific arguments and articles are not intelligible to everyone, and such information is very practical for business people. It seems to me that if we have more open discussions, we will have more supporters for the ecological movement."

As for my own opinion, I believe that when our thinking about nature becomes less utilitarian and we understand its intrinsic value, we will better appreciate the words of a boy from Kalinykia: "I am against, against, and once more against the fact that we have no flowering steppe in the spring and I cannot see tulips with my friends!"

Translated by Yelena Gurvich

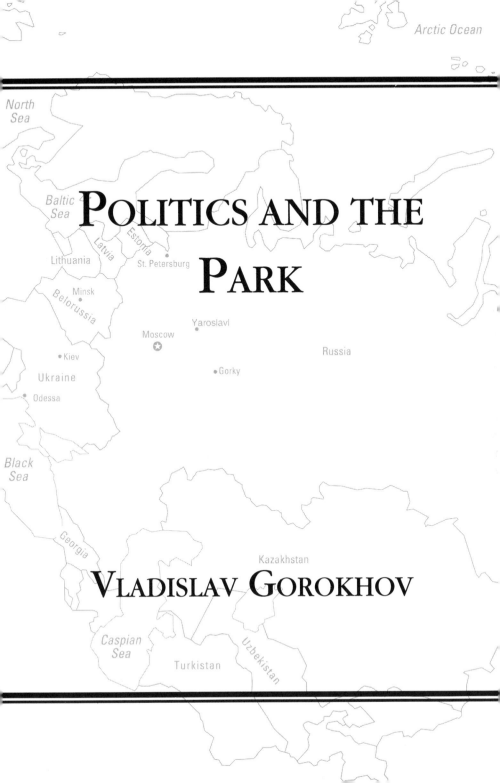

POLITICS AND THE PARK

VLADISLAV GOROKHOV

Mr. Gorokhov, seated far right

V ladislav Gorokhov was born in Bikin in far eastern Russia. He was raised in Moscow and received an engineering degree.

Mr. Gorokhov is a member of the Supreme Soviet, the Soviet legislature. He is also a leading specialist on Soviet national parks and director of Elk Island National Park in Moscow. He is a regular contributor to Soviet newspapers and periodicals and the author of more than twenty books on environmental issues. He has traveled extensively.

Mr. Gorokhov lives in Moscow.

T he history of Elk Island National Park in the 20th century exemplifies the strong tie between politics and the environment in the Soviet Union. Located in Moscow, Elk Island is composed of territory from three city parks and five suburban parks. The dramatic transition now occurring in the USSR is affecting the park and the environment as a whole, introducing new threats, uncovering damage that was previously concealed, and recasting the role of the Soviet environmental movement.

The idea of designating Elk Island a national park was first proposed in 1912, during the reign of Tsar Nicholas II. At the time, Russia was a semi-feudal nation; 80 percent of its population comprised peasants who did not own the land they tilled.

Two years later World War I broke out, with grim consequences for Russia. Three years later, in February 1917, Tsar Nicholas II was deposed. His government was replaced by a weak provisional government which was itself overthrown nine months later by the Bolshevik (later Communist) Party. Civil war broke out as rival groups fought for control of the country. Two years later, in the midst of these years of national upheaval the question of Elk Island was understandably shelved, not to be raised again at the highest levels of government for sixty-six years.

When the idea was again proposed in 1983, a year after the death of Leonid Brezhnev, General Secretary of the Communist Party, the subsequent chronology of events paralleled those of 1912 and thereafter. Two years later, in 1985, Mikhail Gorbachev ascended to power in the midst of a crisis of confidence over the long-term viability of the

Soviet system, and in 1988 another revolution occurred in the USSR, an economic revolution.

This time, however, the political and economic turbulence in the country did not preclude the establishment of Elk Island as a national park. It was officially designated in 1983.

In specifying the year in which Elk Island was made a national park I do not mean to suggest that the process occurred overnight. As early as the 1960s Soviet scientists and some segments of the public revived the issue of Elk Island, at which time the idea of making it a national park was introduced on a popular level. This notion was proposed to a Soviet citizenry indoctrinated for forty years in the ideal of internationalism. Not surprisingly, puzzled citizens protested: "What do you mean by 'national' park? We are *inter*nationalist!" It was difficult to overcome this notion, so long fostered among the Soviet people.

The powerful and strongly conservative segment of government known as the Soviet bureaucracy also resisted the idea of creating Elk Island National Park. In fact, I knew several people who worked on behalf of Elk Island whose diligent efforts to overcome deep-seated bureaucratic inertia were so taxing and ultimately ineffective that they resulted in the loss of their health or left their careers in ruins.

Over the next several years, however, environmental activists gradually influenced public opinion by means of press, radio, and TV. In the 1970s, in fact, their most compelling public statements about ecological damage and the need to preserve the environment were adopted by governmental and Communist Party representatives and became the basis of official ecological resolutions. These pronouncements from the Kremlin confirmed that those in power were tackling the issue and were committed to change. Environmental abuses would be stopped, future injury prevented, and the environment preserved.

But by the beginning of the 1980s Soviet environmental policy had proved to be a sham. Corruption and bureaucratic inertia had enervated the enthusiastic decrees of the 1970s and rendered official efforts stillborn. Intentionally or otherwise—through greed, incompetence, negligence, or the miasma of stolid hopelessness that so marked the official machinery of Soviet bureaucracy—the fate of all these "green" resolutions was the same: They were discussed and developed over a long period, announced with pomp and circumstance, and subsequently if quietly shelved.

One cannot say that the environmental resolutions were mere fictions. But for Soviet policymakers the environmental movement was little more than a whim, an arrogance. At the time the word "plan" still connoted magical properties, promising unrealistic abundance, premiums, and prices. There were five-year plans, annual plans, national and republic plans, and the corresponding production targets were always achieved on paper if not in fact.

But the implementation of environmental policies in the real world, rather than merely on paper, required effort: the completion of multiple bureaucratic forms, the securing of signatures of all relevant administrators, the cooperation of those who would actually implement the plan of action, the energy to overcome unforeseen obstacles. Few bureaucrats were willing to invest the additional energy or to risk their status and privileges in order to execute environmental policy. Moreover, Party operatives further hampered its implementation. Like the government bureaucrats, the *apparatchiki** were disinclined to

---

apparatchik—member of the *apparat*, or Communist Party bureaucracy.

promote change or take a risk if it threatened their own positions. Generally speaking, this was a period note-worthy for its stagnation, the period from 1964 through 1982 during which Brezhnev was the leader of the Soviet Communist Party.

Meanwhile, the air, land, and water were being polluted. Soviet citizens began to notice the appearance of diseases that could be traced to pollution. That was the true begin-ning of the popular environmental movement in the USSR.

In 1986 the Chernobyl tragedy occurred. It shockingly illustrated to the nation and to the world the poverty of Soviet environmental protection. It also triggered citizen participation never before seen in the USSR. In the summer following the disaster at the nuclear power plant some 170,000 volunteers labored, at risk to themselves, to reclaim the nearby territory, recultivating land, cleaning streams, and planting trees. But their efforts did not stop there. Ecology clubs sprang up with their own special programs, public debates, and information exchanges. They featured speakers, among them many high profile scientists, writers, and public figures. Environmental fever spread across the country, making citizens aware of the foolhardiness of passively waiting for someone else to act.

Moreover, any citizen hoping that managerial and governmental personalities who had figured in previous ecological disasters would repent and pay their debt to society was sooner or later disabused of the notion. The Soviet administrative system was so organized that culpable bureaucrats could be smoothly transferred from one office to another and into a different ministry, bureau, or department, secreted away from public retribution with no one the wiser. In short, no one could ever be held responsible for the careless or intentional destruction of rivers, lakes, fertile land, and even seas like the Aral.

The phenomenon of environmental volunteerism soon spread to Elk Island. It took on a particularly mass expression in this case both because of its proximity to Moscow (with its large numbers of ecologically minded students) and because, in the atmosphere of increased ecological awareness, the polluted condition of the park was discussed widely in the media. Soon environmental specialists—biologists, physicians, and chemists—as well as housewives, teachers, pensioners, and workers, and members of the military rallied around the park clean-up effort. Volunteers consolidated their efforts to address particular problems, such as cleaning up a river, a section of forest, a stand of trees, or sometimes just one tree. In addition, many groups of energetic, educated, and persistent citizens sought political solutions and pressed their local elected officials to reform park policy. Elsewhere, public protest on behalf of the environment resulted in significant victories, such as halting construction of the Crimean nuclear power station.

This display of ecological activism was not universally embraced, however. Some local officials, members of the old guard, attacked volunteers and supporters of Elk Island with the tired and toothless charge of "selfish localism." In the past such criticism would have carried some weight, but in an age of elected representatives and public accountability it was viable only to the degree that it reflected public opinion. When environmental proponents succeeded in stirring up strong public support, their recent opponents turned coat and joined forces with them. They scrambled aboard the politically correct bandwagon and participated in the final stage of the clean-up in an attempt to erase the memory of their earlier condemnation of environmental activism, so out of step with public opinion.

The environmental movement, whose emergence had been fostered by perestroika, was now testing the limits of the citizens' ability to affect policy. Generally speaking, elected local officials were responsive. They had already begun to fulfil willy-nilly the demands of their constituents

147

in Moscow and its suburbs, whatever those demands might be. They began to support actions sponsored by the ecological community because of pressure from their constituencies and they predictably addressed first and foremost environmental concerns in their own districts. The slogan "All power to the soviets!"*, the rallying cry of the Bolshevik Revolution seventy years before, had inspired Party support in many Russians. This paper principle and the public participation it implied had now come full circle and was being used in support of the environment.

But in contrast to their reception at the local level, environmental activists seeking to clean up Elk Island found the members of government ministries and the *apparatchiki*, neither of which was accountable to an electorate, far less responsive. Only small concessions were granted on behalf of the park. The most significant of these concerned the construction of a factory in the park. Air and water filters were added to the plant and its production capacity was reduced, thus somewhat lessening the output of pollutants. The factory was completed by fair means or foul over the protests of environmental activists and despite the fact that the project was in the red even before construction was finished.

As director of Elk Island, I focus my attention on the problems of the park, but I also consider the future of the USSR as a whole. Perestroika and the flowering of a democratic culture have created new opportunities here. Perestroika has increased personal autonomy, multiplied the possibilities available to citizens, and made innovation easier. It has simultaneously opened the door to abuse by opportunists. Some of the young, energetic, and enter-

---

*soviet—Russian for "council." In the slogan it refers to people ruling themselves by means of democratic councils or committees.

148

prising people who have come to power in the Soviet Union are primarily concerned with securing their own advantage.

The future of Elk Island was complicated in 1990 by laws passed by the Soviet legislature granting greater autonomy to local officials. These leaders immediately perceived that their expanded powers would allow them to line their pockets at the expense of the public and the environment, quickly and with impunity, by selling off public timber and land on the sly. Elk Island is a desirable piece of real estate, and its sale could result in a substantial sum of money. That is why efforts to sell it—and counterefforts to prevent its sale—are so vigorous. Elk Island is particularly vulnerable to the machinations of local politicans because each of the parks of which it is composed is under the jurisdiction of a different local official. If any one of these eight officials independently chooses to compromise the park under his or her jurisdiction, the environmental effect will extend to Elk Island as well.

In this period of radical change, old regulations have faded and few new laws have replaced them. In the vacuum, democracy has frequently been supplanted by permissiveness. This too has resulted in uncertainties for the future of Elk Island. One attempt was already made to transfer the park to the jurisdiction of agricultural cooperatives, which probably would have sold the land; fortunately, the move was thwarted by municipal law.

The nation is currently undergoing a wrenching transition from a socialist economy of state-run enterprises to a more capitalist-oriented economy with privately owned businesses. Environmental protection laws have virtually disappeared in the face of new financial plans. Elk Island is one of the first victims of the shift in priorities. Local industrial plants spew pollutants into the air above the park and pour effluents into the river, adversely affecting wildlife and plant life and, of course, making it a less pleasant place for urban dwellers seeking to escape to a pristine spot of nature.

But the critical situation now facing the USSR is in keeping with our historical pattern of development: We endure times of turbulence that strain every nerve, but they always result in a significant step forward for the nation. I am not alone in the opinion that we are creating a genuinely constructive society. I recall this historical pattern of tribulation followed by progress, because the fate of the environmental movement in general and of Elk Island in particular is closely tied to the remarkable changes occurring in government and to the shifting political, economic, and military identities of the former republics of the Soviet Union.

The outcome of the political and economic crises that rock our nation in this trying time of transition cannot be predicted. But the new laws passed, the new political mechanisms put in place, and the new mindset of speaking candidly about problems and of adopting a culture of democracy, all of which have developed over the course of the last six years, will, one hopes, not easily be reversed. Elk Island, which has withstood the turbulence of the past seventy-nine years, will, it is hoped, survive these times intact.

Translated by Yelena Gurvich

THE TEMPORARY
MIRACLE OF THE
SAHEL

BUNMI MAKINWA

B unmi Makinwa was born in Ilesha, Nigeria. He received a master's degree in philosophy at the University of Ibadan, Nigeria, and diplomas in the German language at the University of Saarlandes and the Goethe Institutes in Germany. He has traveled extensively throughout Africa, Europe, and North America.

Mr. Makinwa has been a journalist for the News Agency of Nigeria and was science editor for the Pan African News Agency in Senegal. He is currently a consultant for press and information activities at the World Health Organization in Brazzaville, Congo.

Mr. Makinwa currently lives in Brazzaville with his wife, Olajobi, and three children, Nkrumah, Funmilayo, and Thiat.

A brown hardy goat ran out of nowhere. Nothing pursued it, at least not that I could see. It kept running, darting through the brown stumpy growths that dotted the landscape, until it disappeared into the nowhere it came from. Or it may have merely merged again into the dusty West African landscape, swallowed up in the increasing distance from the moving bus in which I sat.

Perhaps the goat, suddenly aware of its aloneness, had begun to seek company in this vast nothingness. Endlessly the land stretched on—a golden yellow carpet of dust dotted with occasional toughened vegetation. Is there any human life here?

As if to answer my question, three human forms emerged in the distance. Two little boys were crouched and a third, dressed in a pair of shorts and a *boubou**, was gently, absentmindedly hitting a shrub. He was smiling. One of the others jumped up and chased him, and as they ran, numerous goats scattered. I realized that the boys were tending a flock. But with no hut in sight on the barren landscape, it was difficult to imagine where these children lived, what they ate.

On board the bus, I and fourteen other journalists from national and international media were on a sponsored trip to visit several international cooperation projects in Senegal, in West Africa at the eastern edge of the sahel.

"Sahel" is an Arabic word denoting the fringe of a sea or desert. The West African sahel, lying between desert and savannah, has poor soil, sparse prickly vegetation, and a tropical climate characterized by eight to ten months of hot, dry weather and irregular rainfall. Every ten to twelve

---

*boubou—small shirt-like dress commonly worn in West Africa.

years a full drought sets in for several years. Great numbers of animals perish while heading south for food and water; people suffer food shortages and even famine. Stretching 2,500 miles north-south and 1,300 miles east-west, the sahel spans five countries and is almost uniformly flat. Our hosts from the Japanese embassy were going to expose as a lie the oft-expressed idea that "nothing *green* can come out of the sahel." They would demonstrate how they had been able to give a new lease on life to that hot semidesert stretching across the northern belt of West Africa.

Our group had started its journey in Dakar, the capital of Senegal, the previous day. We had arrived in St. Louis, the original capital, last night and had found conditions there to be much like those in Dakar. Our hosts had already informed us, in writing and orally: "We shall stay overnight in St. Louis and then early the next morning we'll continue to the village of Thiago, near Richard Toll, to see our most fascinating project." We were now making our way there. Our bus had left St. Louis barely half an hour ago.

The two-day journey could not have come at a better time. I had taken up appointment with the Pan African News Agency based in Dakar only three months before. Senegal was a brand-new country for me in many ways. I was discovering a culture of a people whose country and mine, Nigeria, are separated by seven other countries although we share the same subregion. Like most sahelian countries, Senegal is agriculturally poor, although the Senegal valley to the south is relatively fruitful. Nonetheless, produce from the south rarely reaches the north because of civil disaffection and the resultant fighting between southern separatists and the government. Driving through the barren sahel, I could appreciate why the Senegalese have an age-long tradition of migrating abroad.

The trip north was also an opportunity for me to stay for two days with people who speak only French, the official language, and one I had studied so much in school but had used so little. I would be seeing not only St. Louis, but also Richard Toll, the last post before the border between Senegal and its northern neighbor, Mauritania.

Despite my enthusiasm as I had boarded the bus, I could not shake my skepticism about international aid. I had observed that more often than not international assistance, particularly official assistance, has satisfied and promoted the interests of the provider rather than addressing those of the recipient. What has accrued to the latter has been only marginal, as the assistance has not been aimed at enabling the recipient nation to become self-sustaining. At best it has been mere welfarism and reinforced the dependence of the receiver on the provider. In my several years of observing international aid projects, I had not observed one in which a genuine transfer of technology had occurred. I did not expect to find the Thiago project any different.

International aid from Japan started flowing into Africa a decade ago. From our hosts we learned that Japan had provided Senegal with a sophisticated new television studio that would soon be put into commission in Dakar. It had also provided Senegalese youths with new technology at a modern educational institution, also in Dakar. We had visited those yesterday.

In Thiés, a fairly big town some 50 miles from Dakar, we had also visited motorcycle-riding international aid workers from Japan, who were laboring in the blistering February heat to nurse seedlings of various food plants before they were transferred to local farmers. Some farmers, we saw, came eagerly to collect these special varieties that would produce greater yields than the traditional ones.

In one of the nurseries we were shown how a regular supply of water was assured for the little plants with a simple and well-constructed water pump. The rows of seedlings were so straight and the plants so perfectly spaced they might have been measured every inch as the seeds were planted. I could not but wonder whether the farmers in Thiés could grow their plants and crops this way, and whether they would be able to obtain regular supplies of fertilizers and water to keep their future seedlings so healthy.

The seedlings, we were told, would give fatter crops and yield bigger harvests. They were being offered free. For as long as they were available they were the best, and among the farmers it was fashionable to obtain these modern and foreign products. The latest. Maybe one or two farmers would even be able to maintain the quality.

Afterward, during the long ride north from Thiés to St. Louis, we had seen the few trees and green vegetation by the roadside gradually turn into shrubs. The road was smooth, but the traffic decreased as if even the vehicles wanted to be spared the heat. Occasionally a cluster of huts appeared on the far edge of the increasingly dry and flat landscape. From time to time I caught a glimpse of a city. The bus passed billboards that promised the good life: a good meal, cold drinks, and air-conditioned rooms for unspecified fees. Just like anywhere in the world.

Now, as we made our way to Thiago, a few "skyscraper" vehicles swung dangerously as they yielded some little space for our speeding bus to pass them. Mauritania must need many things from Senegal; how else could one explain the towering northbound loads, measuring some two yards above the upper rim of the uncovered lorries and buses that we passed?

As more of the sahel opened up I noticed the absolute dryness. The last rain, when there is any in this part of Africa, comes in August, sometimes September. During our visit in February, therefore, no drop of water had fallen on the land for five months. With a noon temperature of above 48° Celsius (118° Fahrenheit) in the shade, the land looked dead. Part of the time I saw miles of sheer nothingness, of caky brown surface that merged with the white sky at an undefined point.

Naturally, I made comparisons with the place I knew best. In southwestern Nigeria, where I was born and raised, people talk only of the rainy season and the dry season. There is no third season. Farmers talk of "too much rain this year," and in another year they talk of "too little." They even say, "Oh, how good it would have been if these rains had tarried a little and would fall in the coming months."

Rains sometimes determine the daily schedule. "I'll come over to see you if it does not rain," someone may say, looking at the overcast sky.

"You cannot go to school today. This rain is so heavy it can exhume the corpse of a lazy person," my grandmother used to say to me when I was an innocent child and would rather have had the schoolteacher keep his worldly knowledge to himself. Then I would roll over in bed, cover my head with the thick cover, and sleep soundly to the music of the rain on the roof.

The children tending goats in the scrub land half an hour outside of St. Louis had probably never heard the music I recalled as I drifted into my memories. I wondered how they would react if they experienced the seven-day rains, the period in mid-August when it rains for days on end.

Our bus continued to devour the long road as my thoughts came in tumbles.

We had passed Richard Toll and were going through the most severe part of the sahel in Senegal. The dryness was so constant it was becoming boring. Like most things, the newness was already fading and the latter tastes were no longer quite as shocking as the first.

Then we came upon it. Abundant greenness broke the rhythm. Lush green vegetation. Plants that grew to the height of a man and more. And they stretched on with the same relentlessness as the earlier dryness. The plants were indeed real, even though they appeared artificial in this particular setting.

On both sides of the road, signposts proclaimed what organizations, governments, or institutions had cooperated to create the miracle. "XYZ Foundation—Senegal Project," "ABC Corporation Assisted Gardening in Cooperation with the Government of Senegal," etc.

"We are now in the village of Thiago," one of our hosts announces, "Just around the corner is the joint Japan-Senegalese project." We have arrived.

The announcement did not come too soon. We had already turned off the highway, and the luxuriant, mouth-watering crops in the fields would have made any farmer smile. Tomatoes, onions, cabbages, and many other crops were growing to sizes I had never seen or even imagined possible. The explanations followed. The Japanese expert was first:

"Senegal currently imports virtually all of its onions, but if we were to go by this example, and if this can be transferred to farmers successfully, it is clear that importation should no longer be necessary."

It was needless for him to say that. One onion and one tomato from this farm would be enough, add a few other ingredients, to make a rich Senegalese stew for a family of six. "The Japanese and American varieties that have been tried here have responded very well and given maximum yield," the expert continued.

Next, the Senegalese government representative briefed us: "The tomato has been found capable of growing here twice a year, yielding thirty-five tons per hectare, an improvement of ten tons per hectare over the traditional system." It all looked miraculous. Everything seemed possible. But how was it done?

"The key factor is mastering the soil and obtaining a regular supply of water," he added. "For the first time in this area, the project has succeeded in growing and harvesting rice, the number one Senegalese staple." The international aid workers were eager to talk of the harsh soil they had encountered and the green belt we now saw. The tour guides and embassy officials enthusiastically discussed how it was possible to make the sahel fruitful. Everyone had something remarkable to say.

We continued the tour, over bumpy and dusty roads, to various farm locations. One of the numerous four-wheel-drive station wagons used for the project led the way. Many of the technical experts, not be outdone, followed the convoy on their motorcycles. The motorcycles themselves presented quite a spectacle—bone-rattling contraptions, they bumped almost happily along the roads. Their riders were completely covered with dust, but it did not matter; there was a show going on, and this rare visit from the outside world had to be celebrated.

And we formed quite an impressive bunch. There was a television camera and an attractive lady from the national television station whose microphone was never more than two inches from any speaker's mouth. Three or four other journalists hung their cameras in various positions on their bodies. From time to time they would turn them upon some person, who would rearrange his or her looks or expression to make sure the equipment recorded a positive image. The portable tape recorders ran noiselessly, their visibility enhanced by the names of their various Japanese manufacturers printed boldly on them. Every speaker got the whole works: The television camera purred softly recording sound and image, the click-click of the cameras confirmed the eternity of the moment, and the scratch of

ballpoints on notebooks seemed to insist on the importance of each particular word.

"We have no problems with the taste of these things at
all." Someone translated the answer of an elderly man, the
spokesman for the farmers of the village. "Indeed, even the
food sellers who buy our harvests have said the taste of
our current produce is better than that of the former
produce. Food has also become cheaper in our village
because our prices remain the same but the produce is now
much bigger. We get seedlings free from these white men,
and our crops grow to these heights," he said, using his
arm to demonstrate.

"But how do you get water to irrigate the crops on your
farms?" a reporter asked insistently. "The aid workers can
do this on their experimental farms using their long pipes
and pumping machines."

"Before these white men came with their ideas, we used
to farm only near water sources. We dug canals that take
water from these sources to the farm beds. When we pour
water from the sources into the canals, the water runs
down the ridges and our crops get enough water."

"You seem to have a long dry season here. What do you
do when there is no rain and even the water sources dry
up?"

"It depends. Some years when it rains well and the
ground is wet, we dig holes and reach water. The children
and women fetch this water and pour it on the farm beds.
We pour the water right close to the crops and that way
the crops get enough water. You see, millet and sorghum
do not need too much water. As a matter of fact when it
rains too much, the insects or locusts come and eat up all
the crops."

"So you don't really want plenty of rain for the millet
and sorghum because of locusts. But you need rain so you
can grow all these new crops, don't you?"

The old man smiled faintly: "What do we want to do with the rains?" he asked. "Normally, during the year and at the right time, we have enough rain for the sorghum and millet to grow well. That is enough. When there is too much rain all other unwanted plants grow and bring grasshoppers and locusts. *Dedeht**,*" he said emphatically.

"You said all the crops on these experimental farms now grow well on your own farms too. How do you get the water to make them grow there?" a reporter cut in skeptically.

"Ask them," the old man replied, indicating the Japanese experts.

"We do not understand. What do you mean?" asked the puzzled reporter.

"I mean ask them where *they* get the water. We now have our farms near their water sources, and they always have water there. That is what we use. And they give us fertilizers too, and insecticides to protect these crops against insects."

The explanation that we finally got from the aid workers was that water for the project comes from a stream some half a mile away through a complicated assemblage of pipes and pumps. A pipe was sunk into the ground so that when the stream was dry water could be pumped from deep wells. What was not immediately apparent was that the local farmers would have to come up with the staggering sum of $50 million to maintain the Thiago miracle on their own.

Dusty but satisfied, the reporters and their hosts board the bus for the long return journey to Dakar. A few kilometers of the Thiago green miracle roll by, and then the everlasting emptiness returns. "The bottom line is to find how

---

dedeht —"no" in Wolof, the national language of Senegal.

to transfer this experiment successfully to the locals," the Japanese coordinator of the project had told a reporter in a one-to-one discussion. And the phrase kept recurring, again and again, until it became a refrain.

Now the scenery has changed and the green farms are far behind. The yellow and brown land has resumed its domination of the landscape, and Thiago and the project seem like a faraway dream. An occasional cluster of huts confirms that human life coexists with the animals. And the shrubs show that, apart from goat meat and milk, some vegetation grows to support life.

The boys who run among the goats here have probably never heard of the green miracle of Thiago. If they had, they might have abandoned their huts and goats to live on those green farms. They might have left millet and sorghum flours for rice and green vegetables. If they had, they would probably also have preferred the taste.

The "Thiago miracle" started three years ago and has resulted in many changes. In Thiago there is now much more to eat, and even the menu has changed. The people still make many meals from millet and sorghum, but now they have rice. With the tomatoes, cabbages, and onions a rich stew accompanies the rice. It is faster and easier to make, and it tastes so good. The children really do not want anything else; if only they could have rice for breakfast, lunch, and dinner.

The times are changing and there is something to be happy about. It is being said that many people will soon start to go to Thiago to buy produce that they cannot grow in their own towns and villages. Maybe it will even become a city, a market crossroad that will serve Senegal and neighboring Mauritania, only four kilometers away. As long, that is, as the Japanese aid workers do not leave.

Bibliography

Commoner, Barry. *Making Peace with the Planet*. New York: Pantheon, 1990. A review of past efforts to address and control environmental damage done by technological development; an explanation as to what was done incorrectly, and how that must be changed.

Durrell, Lee. *State of the Ark*. New York: Doubleday, 1986. An overall discussion of the conservation front including the Gaia theory and the human impact on ecosystems and plant and animal species.

Fraser, Horowitz, and Tukel, Zawistowski. *The Animal Rights Handbook*. Los Angeles: Living Planet Press, 1990. A comprehensive guide to animal rights from minks to cattle to household pets.

In Praise of Nature. Edited and with essays by Stephanie Mills. California: Island Press, 1990. An anthology of environmental literature including essays by Aldo Leopold, Rachel Carson, John McPhee, and an introduction by Tom Brokaw.

Joseph, Lawrence E. *GAIA, The Growth of an Idea*. New York: St. Martin's Press, 1990. An objective overview of the Gaia theory: the Earth is a single, living organism.

Lewis, Scott. *The Rainforest Book*. Los Angeles: Living Planet Press, 1990. An easy-to-read handbook of tips on how individuals can help preserve tropical rainforests.

Lopez, Barry. *Crossing Open Ground*. New York: Vintage Books, 1989. A collection of essays and articles by the author reflecting on nature, urging respect and admiration for that which is also a part of humanity.

May, John. *The Greenpeace Book of the Nuclear Age.* New York: Pantheon, 1990. An informative record of nuclear accidents and radiation incidents.

McKibben, Bill. *The End of Nature.* New York: Anchor Books, 1989. An exploration of the philosophies and technologies that may render nature a force no longer independent of humanity.

Nichols, John Treadwell. *The Sky's the Limit.* New York: Norton, 1990. A series of photographs of the landscape in New Mexico with comments on pollution, ecology, wildlife conservation, and the exploration of natural resources.

Rolston, Holmes. *Environmental Ethics.* Philadelphia: Temple University Press, 1990. An exploration of environmental values from several points of view including the beliefs of humans as superior beings, of animals as sentient, and of organisms, species, and ecosystems as having intrinsic value.

Scarce, Rik. *Eco-Warriors.* Chicago: The Noble Press, 1990. An examination of the historical background of radical environmental movements, as well as reviews of several groups including examples of their activities, and the future of the environmental movement as a whole.

The Earth Works Group. *50 Simple Things You Can Do to Save the Earth.* California Earth Works Press, 1989. A practical guide to everyday things that individuals can do the help protect the environment.

Zipko, Stephen J. *Toxic Threat: How Hazardous Substances Poison Our Lives.* New Jersey: Messner, 1990. This volume includes information on issues and events such as the Exxon Valdez oil spill, the Chernobyl nuclear accident, the Bhopal pesticide catastrophe, global warming, rainforest destruction, the washing up of medical waste on beaches, and the debate over dioxin in bleached paper products.

Index